More a new Ice Age than global warming

From Mr George T. Paton

Sir, What has happened to the so-called 'greenhouse effect', so widely talked about by prominent scientists for the past few years? May I suggest that we are entering an Ice Age.

Only recently we had the coldest June cricketing day at Headingley since records began (11 deg C). At the beginning of the month we had snow, encompassed with frosts, which have damaged fruit harvests. The sun has disappeared, the temperature remains low, north winds howl and even though it is raining the water tables are still low. All far-reaching from the gobal warming effect we on earth are supposed to have created through polluting the atmosphere.

May I suggest that it is all due to the 'Good Old English Weather Effect', and nothing else?

George C. Paton
Hill Farm
Haversham
Milton Keynes
Bucks

From the *Financial Times*, 22 June 1991

Department of the Environment
Planning Research Programme

L[...]cy

UK [...] ment
an [...] phy

UK [...] ment

April 1992
London: HMSO

ISBN 0 11 752587 1

Cover photograph: Dorset Coast looking East from Lyme Regis   *David Cope*

PREFACE AND ACKNOWLEDGEMENTS

This report presents the results of a six-month desk study of the land use planning implications of climate change, commissioned by the Department of the Environment. It is one of a series of studies, initiated by several government departments and the Economic and Social Research Council, which have examined various aspects of the social and economic implications of climate change. The overall aim of the series was to use existing material to provide conceptual and methodological frameworks for further research.

One of the areas identified for investigation was land use planning and the land use planning system. This report covers two aspects of the relationship between climate change and land use planning. These are:

- the land use planning implications of policies that might be adopted to reduce emissions or atmospheric concentrations of radiative forcing (greenhouse) gases; and

- the land use planning implications of physical impacts of climate change and adaptive responses in the UK.

The aim of the desk study was to provide an overview and to establish priorities, not to undertake exhaustive analysis of all identified land use planning implications. The report is intended to inform and stimulate debate among land use planning specialists and professionals, those responsible for determining policy in this field and those whose activities in other areas may bring them into contact with the land use planning system.

The authors are grateful to the many individuals who have discussed the subject with them at different levels of formality (a list of consultees is given in Appendix 2), to all those who commented on the first draft of this report and to participants in the Seminar held to discuss the second draft in December 1991.

They are particularly grateful to John Zetter of DPS1 division of the Department of the Environment, Chairman of the Steering Group, to all members of the Steering Group and to the Department's nominated officer, Caroline Johnson.

Thanks are also due to the efforts of Dr David Everest, Senior Research Associate of the UK Centre for Economic and Environmental Development and to two of the Centre's research assistants, Richard Cowell and Jo Smith, for their inputs to the study.

The drawing work was done by Ian Agnew and Mike Young of the Cambridge University Geography Department to whom the authors are also grateful.

CONTENTS

		Page No
Executive Summary		viii
Section 1	**Context and Methodology**	1
	1.1 Climate change: the land use planning dimension	3
	1.2 Important themes	5
	1.3 Climate change and the UK	8
	1.4 Responses to climate change	13
	1.5 Methodology and analytical framework	17
Section 2	**Land Use Planning Implications of Impacts of and Responses to Climate Change**	21
	2.1 Introduction: priorities for land use planning	23
	2.2 Coasts	25
	2.3 Transport	35
	2.4 CHP, wind and tidal power	48
	2.5 Passive solar and microclimatic design of buildings	59
	2.6 Further implications: electricity generation, water and recreation	65
	2.7 Agriculture, forestry and nature conservation	75
Section 3	**Conclusions and Priorities for Further Research**	83
	3.1 Conclusions	85
	3.2 Priorities for further research	88
Notes and References		91
Appendices		101
	1. Acronyms	101
	2. List of Contacts	103
	3. Further details on production of climate change scenarios	104
	4. Summary tables of links between climate change and land use planning in initial areas of investigation.	106

TABLES

		Page No.
Table 1	Targets for stabilising and reducing CO_2 emissions from present levels	14
Table 2	UK CO_2 emissions: 1985 figures and future scenarios	15
Table 3	Framework for exploring links between climate change and land use planning	17
Table 4	Selection of policy options	18
Table 5	Responses to climate change with land use planning implications	19
Table 6	UEA Cost-Benefit Analysis: Present value of net benefits of 'active' response strategies – flood and erosion hazard combined, 1990–2050	26
Table 7	Land use bands proposed for defining standards of service for sea defences	32
Table 8	Estimates of energy savings and carbon dioxide emission reductions from modal shift	36
Table 9	Comparison of primary energy consumption for telephone calls and travel	38
Table 10	Influence of land use patterns on energy demand for transport	39
Table 11	Residential densities, automobile ownership and use, and transit use, Greater Toronto Area (Fall, 1986)	43
Table 12	'Realistic' potential for CHP	50
Table 13	Structural variables affecting space heating requirements at the micro-scale	59
Table 14	Comparison between solar and conventional layout	61
Table 15	Means of enhancing microclimate in the spaces around buildings	61
Table 16	Carbon dioxide emissions from electricity generation fuels	66
Table 17	Carbon emissions from current and new generating systems	66
Table 18	Impacts and sensitivities of climatic variability on the water industry's activities	71
Table 19	Adequacy of existing resources in NRA regions	72

FIGURES

		Page No.
Figure 1	Critical time thresholds in relation to research on climate change	7
Figure 2	IPCC scenarios: increases in global mean temperature	8
Figure 3	IPCC and CCIRG sea level rise scenarios	9
Figure 4	CCIRG predicted summer and winter mean temperatures (for 'central England') and distribution of increase gradients	11
Figure 5	Typology of policy responses	13
Figure 6	Examples of 'savings curves' for carbon dioxide abatement options	16
Figure 7	Analytical framework for analysis of land use planning implications of preventive and adaptive responses to climate change	20
Figure 8	Sea level rise: land potentially at risk from flooding	27
Figure 9	Projected global mean sea level rise (cm) and design allowances	28
Figure 10	Coastal zone set back policies in different countries	31
Figure 11	Decision analysis framework	33
Figure 12	Primary energy requirements of different modes of transport	37
Figure 13	Possible trends in traffic and petrol price elasticities over time	39
Figure 14	Gasoline use per capita versus population density, 1980	44
Figure 15	Costs of CHP, small city development with 10% discount rate	52
Figure 16	Comparative scale to illustrate land use implications of on-shore windpower to a significant energy contribution	56
Figure 17	Examples of NRA forecasts of water in relation to supply options	72
Figure 18	Interactions between agriculture, forestry, nature conservation and land use planning	76
Figure 19	Factors affecting energy demand at different scales of development	87

EXECUTIVE SUMMARY

The desk study: objectives and methodology

1.   The physical impacts of climate change, and policies which might be adopted to prevent or adapt to it, have profound social and economic implications. Among these, the effects on land use and land use planning are potentially important but have received relatively little attention to date. This report, the result of a desk study commissioned by the Department of the Environment, is an initial attempt to set out the land use planning dimension of climate change in the UK.

2.   The desk study was based largely on the findings of the UK Climate Change Impacts Review Group. Its main objective was to identify the implications for land use planning of:

- direct effects of climate change on the natural and human environment in the UK; and

- preventive and adaptive policies likely to be adopted in response to climate change.

3.   The aim was to identify ways in which the planning system itself might need to respond to these changes, either in reaction to new pressures or in a proactive mode. Another key objective was to identify priorities and frameworks for further research.

4.   The study was conducted in three phases: in the first a broad conceptual framework was established; in the second, responses and policies with potentially significant implications for land use planning were identified and in the third the links between climate change and land use planning in selected areas were explored in detail.

5.   Not all potential responses to climate change have identifiable land use planning implications. Initially ten areas (including, for example, the transport sector, the coastal zone and the electricity supply industry) where physical impacts or responses might impinge directly or indirectly on the land use planning system were selected for further investigation.

6.   A sectoral approach was adopted, which explored separately the implications for land use planning of responses in the selected areas. In each case the analytical framework allowed for three possible levels of response in order to test the sensitivities of the land use planning system. Particular attention was paid not only to the strength of the link with land use planning but also to the likelihood of policies being pursued and to critical time thresholds. Interactions with the land use planning system were considered in terms of direct land requirements, redistribution of development pressures, mode of planning system response (in particular, the potential to use the planning system as a policy instrument) and the possibility of significant institutional changes involving the remit of the land use planning system and its coordination with other policy areas.

Important themes

7.   A number of important themes link many of the land use planning implications of climate change.

8.   The first relates to the combination of uncertainties which makes the interaction between climate change and land use planning very complex. In particular, the nature and timing of the impacts of

climate change for an area as small as the UK cannot currently be predicted with any confidence and major uncertainties attach both to policy responses and to social and technical change over the long time periods involved.

9. A second important theme is the way in which the threat of climate change acts as a lens to focus attention on issues, such as coastal zone management, which are already of considerable significance for land use planning. In some cases the resulting additional stimulus for new policies and institutional change is likely to be the most important implication for the planning system.

10. A third broad issue is the potential use of land use planning as a policy instrument in preventive or adaptive responses to climate change, for example, as a means of reducing emissions from transport and buildings or of minimising future risk to property in coastal zones. Such considerations raise questions about the effectiveness of land use planning in achieving the desired goals, and about the costs and benefits of using the planning system as opposed to alternative policy instruments. Land use planning as a policy instrument is unlikely to be effective if it is working in isolation, 'against the grain'. For example, location policies which seek to influence travel behaviour may have counter-intuitive effects unless combined with fiscal policies which convey essentially the same message to energy consumers.

11. A final theme relates to climate change as a rationale for policy responses in the land use planning system (as elsewhere). If the threat of climate change diminishes as uncertainties are resolved, policies tied too closely to this issue may be jeopardised, even where they are complementary to other policy objectives. There is a need to maintain a sense of proportion and to consider the full range of costs and benefits associated with different policy proposals.

Land use planning implications of climate change

12. The most significant land use planning implications of climate change arise in two areas: from the increased threat of flooding and erosion in the coastal zone; and from policies which might be adopted to abate emissions of radiative forcing (greenhouse) gases in the transport sector.

13. In the former case, the implications are important because there is some certainty that sea level rise will occur, because if higher predictions are realised there would be increased hazard, increased costs or both and because land use planning has a

potentially significant role both in reactive mode and as a policy instrument for internalising risk. Links with land use planning are strong because of the impact of flood and erosion hazards on land resources and infrastructure, with possible requirements for relocation; because sea and coastal defences have significant environmental impacts (aesthetic and in broader terms, for example on other coastal areas and for materials); and, most importantly, because land use planning might be a key instrument of integrated coastal zone management which could provide the best framework for an adaptive response to sea level rise. There is probably a period of at least two decades in which to gather more information and formulate appropriate policies.

14. In the case of transport, while the likelihood that the sector will bear a substantial share of emissions abatement in the UK is only moderate, the links with land use are so fundamental that the implications for land use planning cannot be ignored. Policies which might be adopted to reduce emissions from the transport sector are amongst those with the most significant implications for the land use planning system. Implications arise from land requirements for transport infrastructure, from the impacts of transport policies on development pressures and from the need to integrate land use and transport planning at all scales, involving closer co-operation between the agencies involved, consideration of development pressures which might arise from transport infrastructure and assessment of the transport implications of new development. In all of these areas there is scope for the land use planning system to be both reactive and proactive. Land use planning is also a potential policy instrument which could be employed to encourage the use of energy-efficient forms of transport and to reduce the need for movement in the medium to long term.

15. Other substantial implications relate to energy supply and demand. The further development of combined heat and power systems, wind energy and tidal power emerged as responses in the electricity generating sector with the greatest potential to impinge on the land use planning system. In relation to energy demand, passive solar and microclimatic design of buildings raises important issues for development control.

16. All of the other policies and responses examined have *potentially* significant implications for land use planning, but for various reasons these were judged to be less immediate and/or less direct than those mentioned above. This does not imply that the links are unimportant or that they do not merit some attention now. However, they will probably not require special responses or initiatives within the land use planning system in the short term.

17. Electricity, water and recreational facilities clearly involve the land use planning system (or closely parallel procedures), and developments have often been contentious. With the exception of the electricity options mentioned above, however, the analysis suggests that links with land use planning in these sectors are not very sensitive to climate change, or that impacts and responses are so speculative that it is difficult to draw meaningful conclusions about their land use planning implications. In the case of the water industry, there are some wider implications for regional planning in areas where climate change may exacerbate an already difficult supply/demand situation.

18. Responses to climate change in the other sectors examined – agriculture, forestry and nature conservation – have relatively few direct or short term implications for land use planning. This is partly because the planning system currently has a limited remit in relation to these sectors, where many changes do not involve 'development'. More importantly, perhaps, the influence of other factors (such as reform of the Common Agricultural Policy) is likely greatly to outweigh that of climate change in the short to medium term. Climate change may, however, serve to focus attention more sharply on existing problems and it could prove to be a catalyst for modification of the remit of the planning system in relation to rural land use change.

Land requirements and development pressures

19. None of the preventive or adaptive responses to climate change have major implications for the land use planning system in terms of significant direct land requirements in the short to medium term, though some might give rise to developments which will be contentious in a site-specific context. Wind power in particular, though unlikely to be implemented extensively on this time scale, raises novel and controversial siting issues. An accelerated shift away from coal-based energy is likely to contribute to the supply of surplus, often derelict, land. Sites could be reclaimed and used for some other, possibly industrial, purpose, but decontamination may be necessary.

20. Certain responses to climate change could lead to a significant redistribution of development pressures. These are most likely to arise from modified travel patterns, planned or unplanned retreat in the coastal zone and the changing geography of opportunities in the agricultural and forestry sectors. While these implications are far from certain, and are only likely to manifest themselves in the medium to long term, they are important because they are potentially of considerable significance for patterns of land use and because the land use planning system itself requires relatively long time scales in which to adjust to new pressures, unless it is to be entirely reactive. These new pressures also have implications for the scale at which the land use planning system operates.

Areas for further research

21. In some areas related to climate change – for example, increased use of renewable resources and location policy to reduce travel demand – the need for planning policy guidance is already apparent. In many cases, the full implications cannot be clarified without further informaton and research. There is still a need for basic theoretical and empirical work. There is also a need to assess current practice, to identify potential constraints on policy development and to explore, at least in qualitiative terms, the relative costs and benefits of using the land use planning system as a policy instrument in the response to climate change. Other key areas for research include international comparative work and analysis of the strongly interrelated nature of some of the effects of climate change which will impinge upon the planning system. Finally, since the threat of climate change alters the context within which the land use planning system operates, there is a need to develop analytical tools to assist planners in the formulation and evaluation of appropriate policy responses.

SECTION 1
Context and Methodology

1.1   Climate change: the land use planning dimension

1.2   Important themes

1.3   Climate change and the UK

1.4   Responses to climate change

1.5   Methodology and analytical framework

1.1 Climate Change: The Land Use Planning Dimension

Introduction

1.1.1   Climate change has been a dominant environmental issue in recent years. The broad conclusion that emissions of radiative forcing gases (rfgs) from human activity are causing an enhanced greenhouse effect has been accepted by governments since the report of the Intergovernmental Panel on Climate Change (IPCC) in August 1990.[1] Though many scientific uncertainties remain, the enormity of the possible consequences has led to mounting political pressure for preventive policies to be adopted in accordance with the precautionary principle. Whatever measures are taken, however, some impacts of climate change now seem unavoidable, because of the long lifetime of rfgs in the atmosphere.

1.1.2   The potential physical impacts of climate change on the natural and human environment fall into two main groups: those associated with climatic parameters (means and extremes of temperature and precipitation, cloud cover, wind, storms etc.), and those associated with rising sea levels. In some circumstances the two will interact, for example, in the case of extreme events such as storm surges. In addition, increased atmospheric concentrations of carbon dioxide may have direct effects on vegetation.

1.1.3   The physical impacts of climate change, and policies which might be adopted to prevent or adapt to it, have profound social and economic implications. Among these, the effects on land use and land use planning[2] are potentially important but have received relatively little attention to date.[3] This report is an initial attempt to set out the land use planning dimension of climate change in the UK. It is based on a desk study, one of the main objectives of which was to establish an agenda for future action and research.

1.1.4   Climate, sea level and atmospheric carbon dioxide concentrations have implications for the land use planning system because of their potential effects on managed and natural ecosystems, existing and planned infrastructure and a range of human needs and activities. As physical impacts manifest themselves, adaptive policies are likely to become necessary in varying degrees. Some will have significant implications for land use planning in terms of development control, environmental impacts and siting requirements. Land use planning is likely to have both a reactive and a proactive role.

1.1.5   Preventive policies also have potential land use planning implications. For example, energy supply mix will influence siting requirements for new facilities; some energy options imply planning constraints (for example, combined heat and power systems and passive solar design); policies affecting the transport sector have planning implications because of land use/transport interactions; and the planning system itself may become a policy instrument in the response to climate change.

1.1.6   The study was not strictly limited by the remit of the land use planning system as defined by the Town and Country Planning legislation. We have considered, for example, developments for which broadly parallel procedures apply. Given the long time scales of climate change, we have also given some consideration to possible future changes to the remit of the current system, for example, in relation to agriculture and nature conservation.

3

Structure of this report

1.1.7 In Section 1, we consider the potential impacts of climate change in the UK, drawing upon the recently published report of the Climate Change Impacts Review Group[4], discuss possible policy responses and outline the methodology and analytical framework used in the desk study.

1.1.8 In Section 2, the land use planning implications of specific responses to climate change are considered in more detail. Initially we selected ten sectors in which physical impacts and preventive or adaptive policy responses might impinge directly or indirectly on the land use planning system. (See Table 5: selection is discussed in Section 1.5). Section 2 is structured to reflect the relative significance of these sectors as revealed by the subsequent analysis of land use planning sensitivities.

Emerging priorities for the land use planning system

1.1.9 The most significant land use planning implications of climate change arise in two areas: from the increased threat of flooding and erosion in the coastal zone; and from policies which might be adopted to abate emissions of rfgs in the transport sector. The introduction to Section 2 explains these conclusions in more detail. Coasts and transport are dealt with in Chapters 2.2 and 2.3 respectively.

1.1.10 Other substantial implications relate to energy supply and demand. The further development of combined heat and power (CHP) systems, wind energy and tidal power emerged as responses in the electricity generating sector with the greatest potential to impinge on the land use planning system: these are considered in Chapter 2.4. In relation to energy demand, passive solar and microclimatic design of buildings raises important issues for land use planning and is dealt with in Chapter 2.5.

1.1.11 All of the other policies and responses examined have *potentially* significant implications for land use planning, but for various reasons these were judged to be less immediate and/or less direct than those mentioned above. The rest of Section 2 is therefore divided into two Chapters. Chapter 2.6 considers sectors in which developments involve the planning system (or closely parallel procedures), but where responses to climate change seem unlikely to have immediate or direct implications for land use planning: it covers responses in the electricity generating sector (other than those mentioned above), the water industry and tourism/recreation. Chapter 2.7 discusses sectors where climate change may have significant implications for *land use*, but in which the land use planning system currently has a limited remit: it deals with agriculture, forestry (including afforestation for carbon fixing) and nature conservation.

1.1.12 Section 3 draws together the conclusions of the desk study and identifies key issues for further research.

1.2 Important Themes

1.2.1 Before outlining the possible impacts of climate change in the UK, we draw attention to a number of important themes which link many of the land use planning implications of these effects.

Uncertainty

1.2.2 The first theme is the pervasive uncertainty which inevitably dominates a study of this kind. Though the literature is extensive, there is a lack of reliable, quantitative information on fundamental aspects of global climate change and other parameters relevant to the study, most importantly:

- the extent and timing of potential impacts of climate change and sea level rise, especially at a spatially disaggregated level; for a specific, and small, geographical area like the UK, it is currently impossible to predict with confidence what the effects might be;

- future social and economic trends (such as locational trends and changes in agricultural policy); and technological developments;

- the nature, extent, timing and impacts of preventive and adaptive responses. Though some policy responses will be discrete and will have visible consequences, others – such as pollution taxes – may take considerable time to work through the economic system and display their full effects;[5] and

- the future level of emissions of rfgs; this will depend on levels of economic growth, fossil fuel combustion and deforestation as well as on preventive policy responses.

1.2.3 It is the *combination* of these uncertainties which makes the interaction between climate change and land use planning so complex. For example, a characteristic of much speculation about the future is that it superimposes changing climate on an otherwise static situation. But changes in society and technology over periods of 50–100 years are likely to be profound: it is necessary only to think back over an equivalent time scale to emphasise this point. Sensitivity analysis can help, but could not realistically be extended to all uncertainties in all areas of investigation within the scope of a desk study.

1.2.4 These uncertainties do not imply that a 'do nothing' option is appropriate for the land use planning system. The long time scales often associated planning policies mean that any necessary responses by the system may need to be considered well in advance of actual physical impacts, and in relation to other critical time thresholds, such as those associated with infrastructure renewal (Figure 1). Furthermore, the timing of both physical impacts and the political responses to them is unpredictable. Change will not necessarily be smooth and continuous; there may be strong pressures for the planning system to react quickly at particular points in time. This implies the need, at least, for a structured analysis of all significant land use planning implications of climate change and an identification of areas where further research is required. The desk study has attempted to meet these objectives and to provide a framework for more detailed information as it becomes available.

A new focus

1.2.5   A second important theme is the way in which the threat of climate change acts as a lens to focus attention on issues which are already of considerable significance for land use planning. In some cases, this is likely to be the most important implication for the planning system.

1.2.6   In spite of great uncertainty, climate change may provide a catalyst for policy change involving the land use planning system in certain areas. Perhaps the best example is in the coastal zone, where the prospect of enhanced rates of sea level rise is adding new impetus to pressures for greater policy co-ordination which have arisen quite independently of climate change. In a similar way, climate change adds a new dimension to important current debates on rural land use change and nature conservation, on the regional implications of water supply constraints and on the potential for greater integration of land use and energy supply planning. If climate change provides a vehicle for reform, the remit of land use planning may be significantly extended in these areas.

The land use planning system as a policy instrument

1.2.7   In a number of the sectors examined in the desk study, the planning system might itself become a policy instrument in preventive or adaptive responses to climate change. It is already discussed, for example, as a means of reducing emissions from transport and buildings, and as a means of minimising future risk to property in coastal zones. These considerations raise questions about the effectiveness of land use planning in achieving the desired goals, and about the costs and benefits of using the planning system as opposed to alternative policy instruments. Such questions are neither new nor specifically related to climate change, but they need to be considered, at least in qualitative terms, even where it is impossible to quantify many of the costs and benefits involved.

1.2.8   Defining the advantages of land use planning policies is particularly difficult when uncertainty is a significant feature of an issue. Though planning is by definition concerned with uncertainty, this problem is presented in an acute form by issues like climate change. Whether location policies will reduce or perhaps even increase emissions from the transport sector, for example, depends on people's propensity to travel, and development control in flood risk areas might incur costs but deliver no benefits if anticipated hazards do not occur.

1.2.9   In such circumstances, decision analysis may provide a useful framework for policy choices and for determining the value of information. It can show how the outcomes of particular decisions – whether or not to impose planning controls, for example – are sensitive to the probabilities of external events, such as sea level rise. We show how such a framework might be developed in the context of development control in the coastal zone in Chapter 2.2 (see Figure 11), but the concept has more general applicability.

A note of caution

1.2.10   A final theme also relates to uncertainties and policy responses. Given the high level of attention commanded by climate change, there is some danger of its over-use as rationale for policy responses in the land use planning system (as elsewhere). Reducing the impact of climate change is often complementary to other policy objectives and it is attractive to use it as an additional argument in the promotion of specific measures. But if the threat of climate change diminishes as uncertainties are resolved, policies ticd too closely to this issue may be jeopardised, even where they are desirable on other grounds. There is a need to maintain a sense of proportion and to consider a full range of costs and benefits associated with different policy proposals.

Figure 1 Critical time thresholds in relation to research on climate change

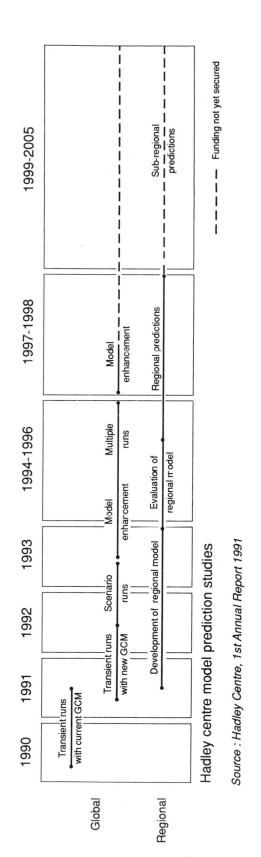

Hadley centre model prediction studies

Source : Hadley Centre, 1st Annual Report 1991

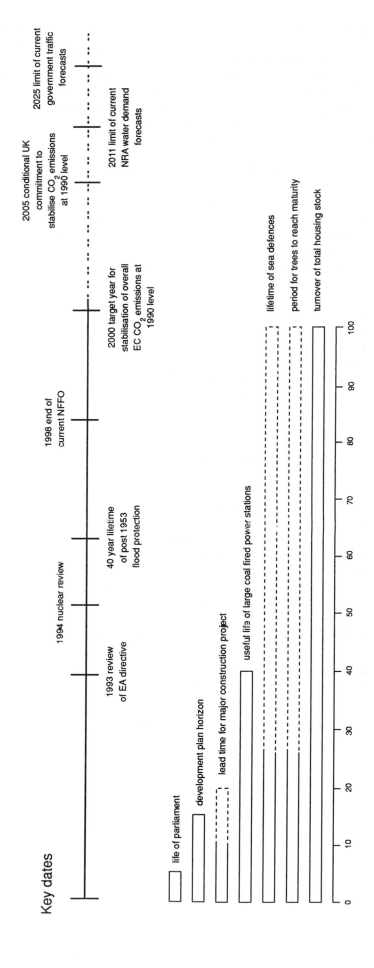

1.3 Climate Change and the UK

Current predictions of climate change and sea level rise

1.3.1 The desk study was based largely on the findings of the UK Climate Change Impacts Review Group (CCIRG).[6] This Group's approach to scenarios of future climatic regimes was similar to that of Working Group I (WG I: Scientific Assessment) of the Intergovernmental Panel on Climate Change (IPCC), which reported in 1990.[7] Both Groups based their findings on the results of general circulation models (GCMs[8]) of global climatic processes. Here we focus on the scenarios of future climate and sea level rise in the UK and on the major uncertainties stressed by both Groups. Further details about generation of the climate change scenarios may be found in Appendix 3.

1.3.2 WG I's findings on global mean temperature increases are summarised in Figure 2. Although an upper and lower estimate was produced for each of the four (emissions) scenarios which the Group considered, the figure shows in each case only the 'best' (central) estimate.

1.3.3 Considerable attention has focussed in the climate change debate on a potential major secondary consequence – rising sea levels, brought about primarily by the thermal expansion of sea water, with the melting of land ice being another contributor.

1.3.4 IPCC WG I considered sea level rise effects resulting from each of its four scenarios. Under its 'business as usual' scenario it predicts an average rate of global sea level rise around 6 –3/ + 4 cm per decade over the next century, to give a predicted total rise above current levels of 20 cm by 2030 and 65 cm by 2100 (Figure 3). Significant regional variations should be expected. WG I considered it unlikely that there would be major impacts during the next 100 years from the large-scale melting of the Antarctic or Greenland ice sheets but noted that these contributed considerably to uncertainty in their predictions.

Major uncertainties

1.3.5 As WG I observe:

'... in their current state of development, the descriptions of many of the processes involved (in GCMs) are comparatively crude. Because of this, considerable uncertainty is attached to these predictions of climate change'.[9]

Figure 2 IPCC scenarios: increases in global mean temperature

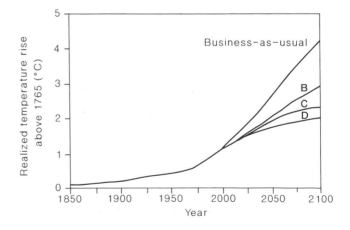

Source : IPCC 1991 (WG 1 report summary), p14

8

Figure 3   IPCC and CCIRG sea level rise scenarios

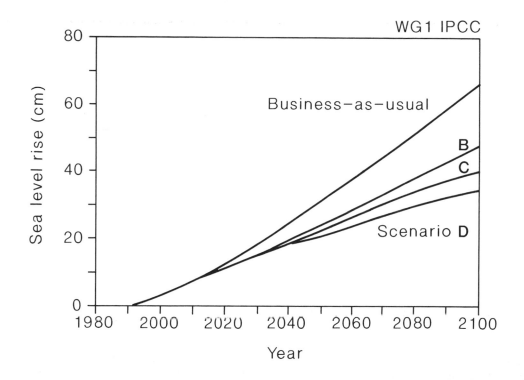

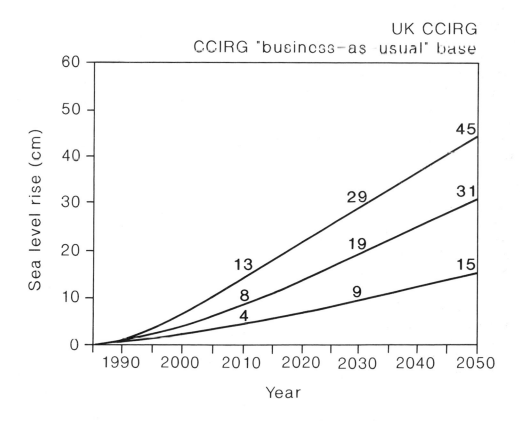

Source : Houghton et al 1990
CCIRG 1991

1.3.6 The climate change research community is now addressing major uncertainties relating to cloud processes and the response of the oceanic system to increased atmospheric carbon dioxide concentrations and to any consequent global temperature changes.

1.3.7 Confidence in regional estimates is particularly low. The regions considered by WG I were large tracts – for example, the 'southern Europe' region stretches from Spain to east of the Black Sea. The British Isles were not included in any area for which regional scenarios were constructed by WG I. The current view of the Hadley Centre for Climate Prediction and Research at the Meteorological Office is that 'there is almost no confidence in predictions for regions smaller than continental scale'.[10]

1.3.8 An important strand of the Hadley Centre's work is concerned with 'regionalisation' and it anticipates making regional predictions during the period 1995–99. Work on sub-regional predictions (and it must be remembered that this is on the scale of distinguishing between Maritime Western Europe [the UK and France together], from a more continental country such as Germany), is scheduled to begin in 1999[11] (see Figure 1). Finer regional distinctions, such as between the UK and France 'will probably still not be possible'.[12]

1.3.9 It is not known when, or indeed if, uncertainties will be resolved by currently planned research. A figure of 15 years for completion was quoted in the 1990 White Paper on the Environment[13] but this would seem to be based on a misinterpretation of the findings of the IPCC WG I which referred to a 10–15 year period in which progress would be necessary merely 'for narrowing the uncertainties'.

Climate change commitment

1.3.10 Because of the lag in the response of the global climate system to increased atmospheric concentrations of rfgs, especially through atmospheric/oceanic interactions, there is some consensus that equilibrium mean temperatures would increase even if all radiative forcing increments ceased immediately. The CCIRG reports that, if the correlation between atmospheric carbon dioxide levels and global mean temperatures over the past 100 years is a causal one, the current levels of atmospheric carbon dioxide imply an inevitable increase in global mean temperature of between 0.6–1.7 deg C before all change is worked out of the system. Other variables, such as precipitation and sea level could be expected to change in harmony with this committed effect.

Implications for the UK

1.3.11 With the above qualifications in mind, we outline the climate change and sea level rise scenarios compiled for the UK by the CCIRG for the years 2010, 2030 and 2050. These were all based on a 'business as usual' emissions scenario.

Temperature

1.3.12 The CCIRG scenarios of seasonal mean temperature increases are shown in Figure 4. The projected summer temperature increase for the country is likely to be close to the global mean and roughly uniform across the country. In winter, the estimates of temperature change show a greater proportionate increase in a southwest-northeast direction. This means that existing geographical differences in winter mean temperatures across the country would tend to diminish.

1.3.13 As well as changes in mean temperatures, the CCIRG attempted to estimate changes in the frequency of extreme events. Mean summer and winter temperature data approximate a normal distribution and, on the assumption that the distribution and its variability remain constant in the climatic transition process, the Group forecast that very warm summers, such as that in 1976, would increase in probability from approximately one in 1,000 to one in 10 by 2030 and one in three by 2050. Similarly, very warm winters, such as that which occurred in 1988/9, would increase their probability from one in 50 currently to one in five by 2030 and one in 2.5 by 2050.

Precipitation

1.3.14 The CCIRG made only very tentative predictions about precipitation changes because of considerable variations in results from the constituent GCMs on which it based its scenarios. The mean result suggested a small increase in precipitation and that the chances of drier summers would be slightly higher in the south than the north of the country. An important consideration is that although there may be zero or positive increases in precipitation, soil conditions may on average become drier, and surface water less, because higher mean temperatures would be associated with greater evaporation.

1.3.15 For winter precipitation, the GCMs used by the Group agreed in the direction of change – towards higher precipitation – though the levels resulting from a doubling of atmospheric carbon dioxide varied considerably. The average figure was + 15 per cent. Time-dependent trend analysis gave best estimates for winter rainfall as a 5 ± 5 per cent

Figure 4 **CCIRG predicted summer and winter mean temperatures (for 'central' England) and distribution of increase gradients**

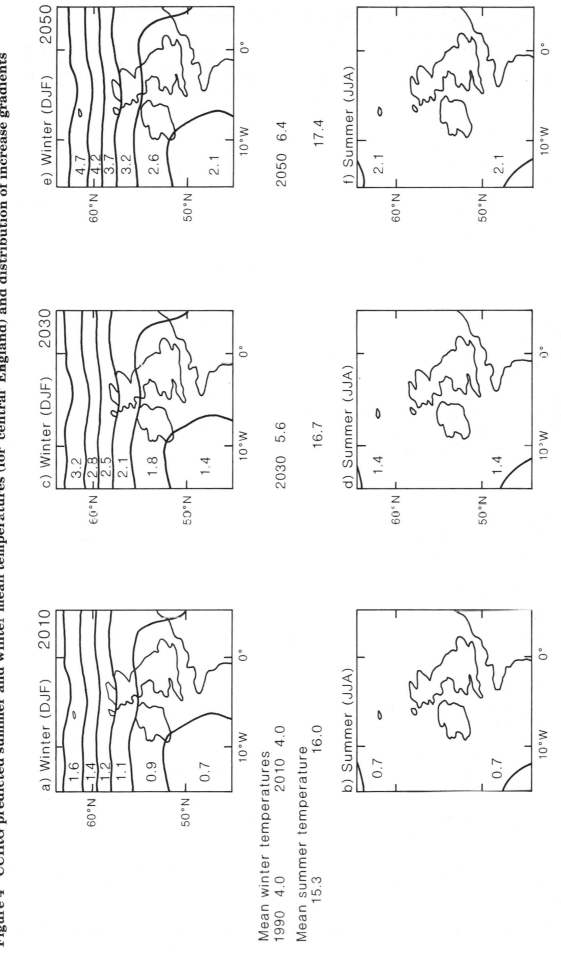

Mean winter temperatures
1990 4.0   2010 4.0   2030 5.6   2050 6.4

Mean summer temperature
15.3   16.0   16.7   17.4

Source : CCIRG 1991

increase by 2030 and 8 ± 8 per cent by 2050. The chances of very dry winters would decline.

Other climatic variables

1.3.16   The CCIRG declined to construct scenarios of climatic factors such as windiness and cloud cover because of the large uncertainties in the models.

Sea level changes

1.3.17   The CCIRG estimates of global mean sea level changes agree closely with the WG I scenarios (see Figure 3).

1.4   Responses to Climate Change

The current policy position

1.4.1   Though there exists a variety of preventive and adaptive responses to climate change (Figure 5), the attention of the international community and of individual countries has tended to focus on the control of rfg emissions, particularly emissions of carbon dioxide.

Targets

1.4.2   Discussion of the need for strategies to control emissions of rfgs dates from at least the late 1960s, but the issue began to receive serious international scientific and diplomatic attention only in the mid-1980s.[14] At the 1987 governing council meeting

of UNEP an agreement was reached to create the Intergovernmental Panel on Climate Change, whose results were reported to the Second World Climate Conference held in November 1990. In 1988, at an international conference in Toronto, convened by the Canadian Government, a call was made for a 20 per cent reduction in emissions of carbon dioxide on 1988 levels, to be achieved by 2005.

1.4.3   Separate from this process, but influenced by it, several countries unilaterally adopted policies on rfg emissions, driven by a growing demand for a 'precautionary approach' to the issue. The official UK policy position was first set out by the then Prime Minister on 25 May 1990. This is concerned only with carbon dioxide emissions:

Figure 5   Typology of policy responses

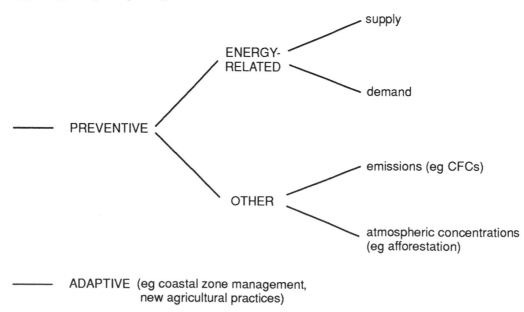

'. . . provided others are ready to take their full share, Britain is prepared to set itself the very demanding target of a reduction of up to 30 per cent in presently-projected levels of carbon dioxide emissions by the year 2005. This would mean returning emissions to their 1990 levels by that date.'[15]

1.4.4   The 1990 White Paper on the Environment[16] suggests that combination of this commitment with existing policies for methane and CFCs would lead to a 20 per cent decline (on 1990 levels) of UK rfg emissions by 2005 in terms of carbon dioxide equivalence. It has never been officially stated what set of circumstances would satisfy the condition of others being ready to take their full share but, as noted below, a number of other countries have adopted targets which are more demanding than those of the UK. The situation is summarised in Table 1.

1.4.5   The next stage in policy development will be associated with the 1992 UN Conference on Environment and Development (UNCED), where the UK is advocating that developed countries should undertake to identify targets and strategies to reduce rfg emissions one year after a general convention is agreed. UK policy is to encourage implementation of emission targets that allow for the radiative forcing effects of all gases, rather than carbon dioxide alone.[17]

1.4.6   Several of the countries listed in Table 1 are members of the European Community. In November 1990, a Joint Council of Energy and Environment Ministers of the Community adopted a target of stabilising emissions of carbon dioxide from the Community as a whole by the year 2000.[18] The Community has been concerned that such a policy should aim at 'eliminating as far as possible the risk of political friction between Member States and dangers for the Internal Market', and has recognised that it will imply adjustment costs 'for some economic agents'.[19] The Council also asked the Commission to prepare, in time for UNCED, 'a proposal for establishing (overall) Community emission reduction targets separately for carbon dioxide and other greenhouse gases, including possible strategy options aimed at progressive reductions at the horizon 2005 and 2010'.[20] The Commission has subsequently published proposals for allocations of national targets for carbon dioxide emissions.[21]

1.4.7   The European Commission has linked rfg emission reduction targets to the improvement of energy efficiency in the Community and has identified a three-year programme of legal actions and standards covering matters such as building energy use, appliance energy efficiency, combined heat and power and motor vehicle performance requirements.[22]

1.4.8   Policies adopted to date have inevitably involved arbitrary percentage emission reductions on levels occurring at various dates in the late 1980s. The efficacy of these reductions in achieving desired alterations to climate change and sea level rise has not been systematically explored in the process of their adoption and, indeed, there has been comparatively little exploration of what the desirable end states and acceptable rates of change in climate and associated variables should be. This issue is now being addressed by follow up work by Working Group II (Impacts) of the IPCC, which is considering the sensitivities of the various sectors affected by climate change.

1.4.9   The current debate is focussed on how international agreement on policies to control rfg emissions can be achieved.[23] The formidable problems which this entails are likely to lead to an incremental approach, with a 'framework' agreement first being sought, seeking to achieve consensus on recognising the problem and the desirability of ameliorative action.

1.4.10   The question of desirable targets, the means of achieving them and the methods of demonstrating compliance with internationally-adopted targets are likely to be postponed for subsequent consideration.[24] Current indications are that any agreements reached will be based on giving individual countries flexibility in determining exactly how to achieve targets and that these targets will be set in terms of rfg 'equivalence' and will not focus on carbon dioxide alone.

Table 1   Targets for stabilising and reducing CO_2 emissions from present levels

Country	Stabilisation	Reduction
Australia		20% by 2005[a]
Austria		20% by 2005
Canada	by 2005	
Denmark		20% by 2000
France	by 2005	20% by 2025
Germany		25% by 2005
Japan	by 2000[b]	
The Netherlands		3% to 5% by 2000
New Zealand		20% by 2000
Norway	by 2000	
Sweden	by 2000	
United Kingdom	by 2005	

[a] All greenhouse gases
[b] Stabilisation of per capita emissions

Source: Resources for the Future

14

Table 2 UK CO₂ emissions: 1985 figures and future scenarios

Central Growth	1985		2005 low		2005 high		2020 low		2020 high	
	MT	%	MT	%	MT	%	MT	%	MT	%
ESI	52	33	67	31	68	33	65	28	90	36
Industry	40	26	56	26	52	25	68	29	65	26
Transport	30	19	49	23	46	23	58	25	54	21
Domestic	25	16	27	13	25	12	28	12	27	11
Miscellaneous	10	6	14	6	14	7	15	6	15	6
Total	158	100	212	100	204	100	234	100	250	100

1 Emissions expressed as million tonnes carbon.
2 All figures rounded.
3 Industry includes agriculture.
4 Transport includes marine bunkers and aviation.

Source: Energy Paper 58

Policy Instruments

1.4.11   Discussion of the instruments for achieving rfg emission reduction targets has focussed on two aspects:

- that the major rfgs are emitted by a wide range of processes critical to the economies of all countries; and

- that the major rfgs are 'uniform pollutants': they have very few local impacts, and their effects are the same wherever on the globe they are emitted. With methane and tropospheric ozone, however, there are non-radiative forcing environmental impacts associated with releases of the gases which might influence the development of policies to control their emission.

1.4.12   There is a considerable body of research on the actual instruments which might be adopted to control rfg emissions, discussing approaches such as 'carbon taxes', the setting of national or regional emissions ceilings, the trading of rights to emit rfgs up to such ceilings, both within and between countries.[25] At present it is not clear which, if any, of these strategies will be adopted, both at the international level and also within the UK as a whole, to achieve its current target for carbon dioxide emission stabilisation. It is increasingly likely, however, that some fiscal measures will be adopted at the level of the European Community, possibly the combined carbon/general energy tax which is favoured by the Commission.[26]

1.4.13   In the case of government policies, the range of possible instruments includes public investment, provision of information, direct regulation and fiscal incentives. There has been growing interest in the use of the price mechanism in environmental policy in the UK, as elsewhere. Instruments relevant to particular policy responses are considered in more detail in Section 2.

Cost effectiveness

1.4.14   The other main thrust of current environmental economics research is to identify options for reductions in rfg emissions in terms of their cost-effectiveness, that is the cost per tonne of carbon dioxide (equivalent) avoided.[27] Though the relative contribution of different sectors to emissions is quite well quantified (Table 2), much work remains to be done on the relative costs of reducing emissions through different measures and using different policy instruments. Research to date has concentrated primarily on carbon dioxide (with some consideration of methane leakage in the power generation sector). Results tend to confirm that improving energy efficiency is relatively cost effective, but are sensitive to the discount rates employed (Figure 6). Additional approaches, such as use of landfill gas or afforestation schemes, have not so far been factored into an overall cost effectiveness analysis in a comprehensive way, nor has the range of potential adaptive policy responses.

Figure 6   Examples of 'savings curves' for carbon dioxide abatement options

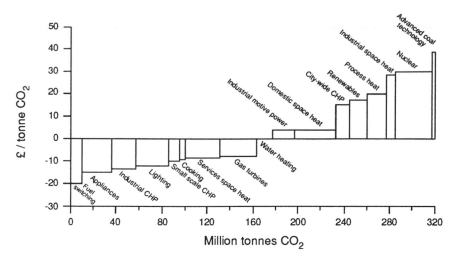

Savings curve for carbon abatement options
(by the year 2005; 10% discount rate)

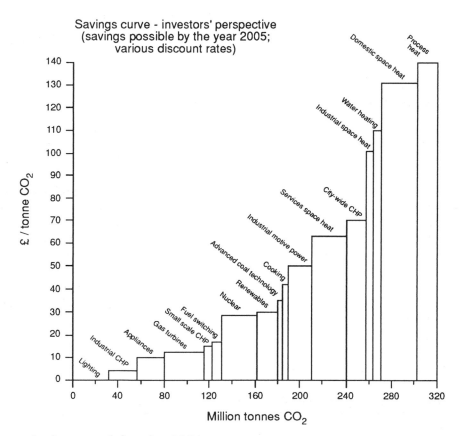

Savings curve - investors' perspective
(savings possible by the year 2005;
various discount rates)

Source : Jackson and Jacobs 1991

1.5 Methodology and Analytical Framework

Methodology

1.5.1 The main objective of the desk study was to identify the implications for land use planning of:

(i) direct effects of climate change on the natural and human environment in the UK ('direct impact effects'); and

(ii) policies likely to be adopted in response to climate change ('policy response effects').

1.5.2 The aim was to identify ways in which the land use planning system might itself need to respond to these changes, either in reaction to new pressures or in a proactive mode, sometimes as a policy instrument. Another key objective was to identify priorities and frameworks for further research.

1.5.3 The study was conducted in three phases: in the first, a broad conceptual framework was established; in the second, responses and policies with potentially significant implications for land use plan-

ning were identified and in the third the links between climate change and land use planning in selected areas were explored in detail.

Conceptual framework

1.5.4 The broad framework adopted for exploring links between climate change and land use planning in the desk study is shown in Table 3.

1.5.5 Implications for land use planning of physical impacts ('direct impact effects') were considered on the basis of a 'business as usual' emissions scenario, that is without any specific preventive policy response except for action on chlorofluorocarbons (CFCs) (left hand side of table). The basis for this part of the analysis was the 1991 Report of the Climate Change Impacts Review Group.[28] The land use planning implications of these effects lie mainly in the adaptive responses[29] which are likely to be made by Government and other agencies and individuals as effects manifest themselves.

Table 3 Framework for exploring links between climate change and land use planning

A. PHYSICAL IMPACT EFFECTS (AND ADAPTIVE RESPONSES)		B. PREVENTIVE POLICY/RESPONSE EFFECTS	
Effects of climate change in UK	Implications for land use planning system	Policy responses to climate change	Implications for land use planning system

1.5.6 The land use planning implications of preventive policy responses, aimed at controlling atmospheric concentrations of rfgs (by reducing emissions or by sequestration), were also assessed. There is interaction between A and B in Table 3, since the more effective the preventive policies, the less the physical impacts are likely to be, reducing the need for adaptive responses. Some effects are already unavoidable, however, because of time lags in the system (the 'climate change commitment'). Thus, for example, many observers consider a sea level rise at least in the lower range of those predicted to be almost inevitable over the next few decades (see Chapter 1.2).

Selection of policy responses for detailed analysis

1.5.7 The translation of broad policy goals (such as reducing emissions or adapting to climate change) into specific policy objectives and instruments is only just beginning. Therefore it was necessary to consider a range of possible policies and responses and then to select those which seemed likely to impinge upon the land use planning system. The analysis included not only the policy framework provided by Government, but also potentially significant policies and responses of other agencies and individuals, such as energy utilities, water authorities and farmers.

1.5.8 The typology of policy responses to climate change which provided the framework for our selection is shown in Figure 5. The range of possible responses is very large and it is clearly impractical to consider the implications for land use planning of all individual policies and policy combinations which could conceivably be adopted over the next few decades. Policies were selected for further analysis by drawing on existing commitments, policy proposals and likely future developments in the UK, the EC and some member states (for example, Denmark and The Netherlands) whose thinking may

become increasingly influential in EC environmental policy over the next decade. The procedure adopted in identifying these policy options is shown in Table 4.

1.5.9 It was clear from our initial analysis of policy responses that many measures likely to be adopted to combat climate change or adapt to its effects have no obvious direct implications for the land use planning system (examples include the phasing out of CFCs and minimum energy efficiency standards for a range of appliances). However, such policies have indirect relevance because some measures are potentially more effective than others (in improving energy efficiency, for example) and the effects of different policies are not necessarily additive.

1.5.10 Effective policies which do *not* have land use planning implications may therefore reduce the significance of policies which do, and in particular may reduce the need for, or potential impact of, proactive measures in the land use planning sector itself. To take an extreme example, if clean and highly efficient vehicles were developed, there might be less pressure to pursue policies which reduce the need to travel, including those concerned with the location of activities. On the other hand, in a comprehensive policy framework, it may be desirable to advance on all fronts so that there is resonance between different kinds of policies with broadly similar aims.

1.5.11 Therefore, while the primary concern of the desk study was with policies with direct land use planning implications, it was necessary to be aware of the effects of a range of other policies which are likely to be adopted.

1.5.12 Policy and responses selected for further exploration are summarised in Table 5.

Table 4 Selection of policy options

IDENTIFY POLICY OPTIONS IN BROAD GROUPS ACCORDING TO TYPOLOGY IN FIGURE 5

↓

FOCUS ON OPTIONS WITH DIRECT RELEVANCE FOR THE LAND USE PLANNING SYSTEM

↓

CONSIDER STATUS OF THESE OPTIONS IN UK, EC AND SELECTED OTHER COUNTRIES

↓

DEFINE POLICY INSTRUMENTS

↓

IDENTIFY MAIN SOURCES OF INFORMATION ON PLANNING IMPLICATIONS OF SELECTED POLICIES

Table 5 Responses to climate change with land use planning implications

PREVENTIVE

ENERGY RELATED
- New strategies in the electricity generating sector (including renewable energy)
- Further development of combined heat and power/district heating
- Policies to reduce emissions from the transport sector
- Policies to improve energy efficiency in buildings through passive solar and microclimatic design

OTHER PREVENTIVE POLICIES
- Afforestation as a means of carbon fixing

ADAPTIVE
- Response to increased flood/erosion hazard in coastal zones
- Response to climate-induced changes in the water supply/demand balance (including saline intrusion and other groundwater changes)
- Changing agricultural and forestry practices
- Protection of notified nature reserves
- New demands for tourism/recreation

Exploring the links between climate change and land use planning: the analytical framework

1.5.13   The object of the study was to explore the *sensitivity* of the land use planning system to a variety of potential preventive and adaptive responses to climate change and to different intensities of response.

1.5.14   In view of the extensive scope of the desk study and the intrinsic uncertainties in many of the key variables, a structured analytical framework was adopted for the exploration of the land use planning implications of the ten selected responses (Figure 7). This framework was intended for use as a guide to thinking rather than for rigid application.

1.5.15   A scenario approach, in which a small number of policy scenarios would be developed at the outset, and their implications for land use planning explored, was considered but rejected. Since the object of the study was to explore the *sensitivities* of the land use planning system to various responses to climate change, such an approach was thought to be unduly restrictive. It would also be very complex to deal with both adaptive and preventive policies in internally-consistent scenarios.

1.5.16   An alternative, essentially sectoral, approach was therefore adopted, which explored separately the implications for land use planning of responses in the ten selected areas. In each case the framework allowed for three possible levels of response in order to test the sensitivities of the land use planning system.

1.5.17   A 'business as usual' level of response was assumed to involve a continuation of current trends and policies. A second level included preventive policies entailing 'no regrets' – measures adopted primarily for reasons unconnected with climate change but which also have rfg abatement benefits – and adaptive responses which attempt to maintain the *status quo* in the face of changing conditions (for example, improved sea defences). The third level – 'enhanced emissions reduction', or 'enhanced adaptive response' – envisaged a situation in which reduction of rfg emissions becomes an urgent policy priority and adaptive responses entail significant changes to the *status quo*, for example major shifts in agricultural zones.

1.5.18   These scenarios were not intended to be precisely quantified; indeed, in most cases, quantification was not practicable within the scope of the desk study. However, they provided a qualitative range of possible response levels and helped to structure the analysis of the land use planning implications of climate change.

1.5.19   In assessing the land use planning implications, the following aspects were given particular attention:

- *likelihood of policy being pursued*, including factors such as contribution to emissions abatement, costs, number of actors involved and political acceptability, and complementarity with other policy objectives;

- *strength of link with land use planning*, for example, in terms of land requirements, effects on development pressures and mode of land use planning system response (reactive or proactive). These criteria are considered in more detail in the Introduction to Section 2;

- *critical time thresholds*; for example, for renewal of infrastructure or diffusion of technologies (such as passive solar design); and

- potential *effectiveness* and *costs* of any planning system response.

1.5.20   Results of applying this framework are considered in detail in Section 2.

Figure 7   Analytical framework for analysis of land use planning implications of preventive and adaptive responses to climate change

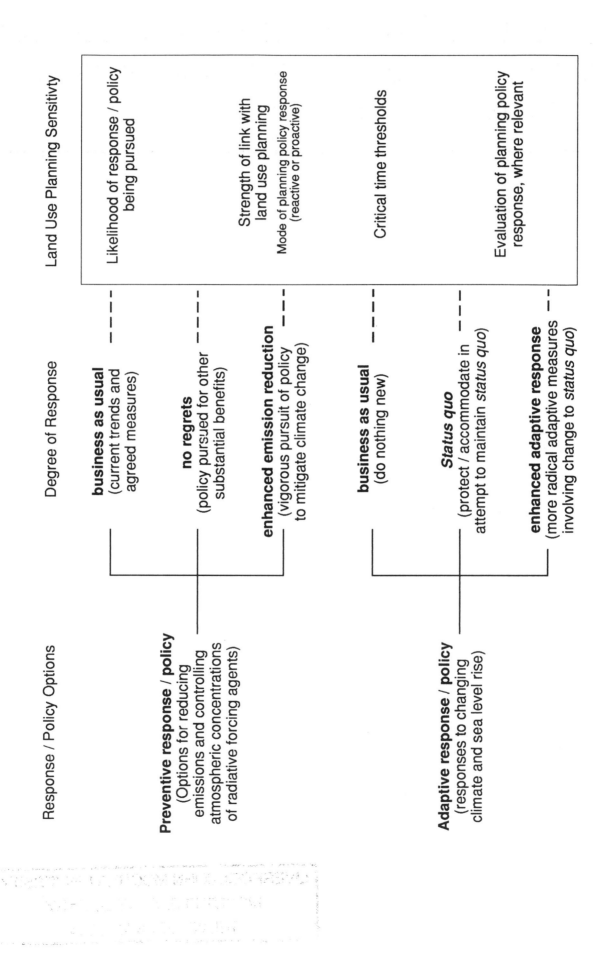

Land Use Planning Implications of Impacts of and Responses to Climate Change

2.1   Introduction. priorities for land use planning

2.2   Coasts

2.3   Transport

2.4   Energy supply: CHP, wind and tidal power

2.5   Buildings: Passive solar and microclimatic design

2.6   Further implictions: electricity generation, water and recreation.

2.7   Less direct effects: agriculture, forestry and nature conservation

2.1 Introduction: Priorities for Land Use Planning

Defining the links

2.1.1 Not all potential response to climate change have identifiable land use planning implications. As outlined in Section 1, we selected ten possible areas where physical impacts and preventive or adaptive policy responses would impinge directly or indirectly on the land use planning system. Even within this selection, results of the desk study suggest that some of the land use planning implications of climate change are more certain, immediate or direct than others. Some policies are more likely to be adopted in the short to medium term, for example, and in certain areas there are very clear and strong links with land use planning. A summary of the implications in the areas initially selected for investigation can be found in Appendix 4.

2.1.2 In defining the strength of the link between preventive or adaptive responses and land use planning, particular attention was given to the following criteria, though these were not used exclusively:

- significant direct *land requirements* (or surpluses) arising in the short to medium term;

- significant *redistribution of development pressures* arising in the medium to long term;

- whether the land use planning system response is likely to be reactive or proactive, and in particular, the potential use of the planning system as a *policy instrument;* and

- the possibility of significant *institutional changes* involving the remit of the land use planning system and its co-ordination with other policy areas.

2.1.3 When all of the above factors are taken into account, an order of priority emerges, as outlined in Chapter 1.1.

Key sensitivities

2.1.4 Of the individual sectors examined, those with the most important land use planning implications are the impacts of sea level rise and adaptive policy responses to the increased threat of flooding and erosion in the coastal zone; and policies which might be adopted to reduce emissions of rfgs in the transport sector.

2.1.5 In the coastal zone, the implications are important because there is some certainty that sea level rise will occur, because if higher predictions are realised there would be increased hazard, increased costs or both, and because land use planning has a potentially significant role both in reactive mode and as a policy instrument for internalising risk. The time scale for change means that there is scope to develop a land use planning policy response. These issues are discussed in Chapter 2.2

2.1.6 In the case of transport, while the likelihood that the sector will bear a substantial share of emissions abatement in the UK is only moderate, the links with land use are so fundamental that the implications for land use planning cannot be ignored. Furthermore, the potential for land use planning to reduce the need for travel and encourage energy-efficient modes is increasingly recognised and has important policy implications. The transport sector is considered in Chapter 2.3.

2.1.7   The other areas with the most immediately significant land use planning implications relate to energy supply and demand – the further development of combined heat and power (CHP), wind energy and tidal power, and passive solar and microclimatic design of buildings.

2.1.8   Only urban-scale CHP has significant implications for the land use planning system and at present the prospects for major development are not strong. However, the potential contribution to emissions reduction is large, the fiscal climate may become more favourable, the viability of CHP is closely related to urban structural variables such as density and mixing of land uses and land use planning might itself influence the feasibility of such schemes.

2.1.9   Of the options for generating electricity from renewable sources, two stand out as having particular significance for land use planning – wind energy, primarily because of its visual impact, and tidal power, because of the substantial environmental and regional planning implications of large-scale schemes. Though the likelihood of major developments in the short to medium term is modest, the links with land use planning in each case are sufficiently strong to merit serious attention.

2.1.10   These three energy supply options are considered in Chapter 2.4.

2.1.11   In relative terms, passive solar and microclimatic design of buildings would make only a small and long-term contribution to reducing emissions of rfgs. But evidence suggests that this might be realised at little or no direct cost. The links with land use planning are crucial because implementation on any signifcant scale would require the active involvement of the land use planning system. These issues are addressed in Chapter 2.5.

Other interactions

2.1.12   All of the other areas examined have *potentially* significant implications for land use planning, but for various reasons they are less immediate, less direct and/or less certain than those mentioned above. This does not imply that the links are unimportant or that they do not merit some attention now. However, they will probably not require significant responses or initiatives within the land use planning system in the short term.

2.1.13   Electricity, water and recreational facilities clearly involve the land use planning system, and developments have often been contentious. With the exception of the electricity options mentioned above, however, the analysis suggests that links with land use planning in these sectors are not very sensitive to climate change, or that impacts and responses are so speculative that it is difficult to draw meaningful conclusions about their land use planning implications.

2.1.14   The electricity supply industry will be an important focus of preventive policies, since it is the largest sectoral source of carbon dioxide emissions in the UK, and a significant source of other rfgs. However, the technologies most likely to be adopted have modest and relatively uncontroversial siting requirements, while technologies with the greatest land take and/or other contentious impacts are less likely to be implemented on a significant scale. CHP, wind and tidal power are exceptions because of their important urban structural, land use and other planning implications.

2.1.15   In the case of the water industry, the potential impacts of climate change are particularly uncertain and its seems likely that other trends and policy developments (for example, the introduction of demand management measures) will have more significant impacts in the short to medium term. There are, however, some wider implications for regional planning in areas where climate change may exacerbate an already difficult supply/demand situation.

2.1.16   Recreation (and tourism) are likely to be affected in a number of ways by climate change, and related developments will almost certainly impinge on the planning system. Climate-induced changes are likely to be long term, however, and difficult to tease out from other trends, so it is possible only to speculate in the broadest terms about their potential implications for land use planning.

2.1.17   These three areas, which involve the planning system directly but where the implications of climate change are difficult to define, are discussed in Chapter 2.6.

2.1.18   Responses to climate change in the other sectors examined – agriculture, forestry, and nature conservation – have relatively few direct or short term implications for land use planning. This is partly because the planning system currently has a limited remit in relation to these sectors, where many changes do not involve 'development'. More importantly, perhaps, the influence of other factors (such as reform of the Common Agricultural Policy) is likely greatly to outweigh that of climate change in the short to medium term. Climate change may, however, serve to focus attention more sharply on existing problems and it could prove to be a catalyst for modification of the role of the planning system. These sectors, which are interrelated in a number of ways, are considered together in Chapter 2.7.

2.2 Coasts

Climate change, coasts and land use planning

2.2.1 Modest rises in sea level, flood and erosion hazards and ways of responding to them are not new issues in the UK. It has long been necessary to make choices about the use of resources in coastal protection and such choices frequently involve conflicting interests. The threat of an enhanced rate of sea level rise draws attention to these choices and conflicts in a more focussed way than has previously been the case.

2.2.2 While it is not possible accurately to assess the assets at risk from anticipated sea level rise, these could be substantial. For example, all of Britain's oil refineries and half of its electricity generating stations occupy coastal or esturial sites; 57 per cent of Grade 1 agricultural land lies below the 5 m contour[30] and many urban and industrial areas together with communications infrastructure are thought to be potentially at risk.[31]

2.2.3 In this Chapter, we consider the potential impacts of sea level rise in the UK, taking account of the current situation, predictions of climate-induced changes in sea level and the enormous uncertainties involved. We outline three possible levels of policy response and then explore in detail the implications for the land use planning system.

Significance for land use planning

2.2.4 Sea level rise, and policy responses to it, have implications for land use planning in a number of ways:

- relocation of infrastructure would have direct land use requirements, and loss of agricultural land might also have indirect implications for land use planning;

- improved and/or new defences have amenity and environmental implications; new defences require planning permission, otherwise local planning authorities are statutory consultees; major works are likely to be subject to Environmental Assessment; and

- development control may have a proactive role; this is currently limited, but might be significantly enhanced if more co-ordinated coastal zone management polices are pursued.

Impacts of sea level rise in the UK

The current situation

2.2.5 The UK has a coastline of about 15,000km. The coast is a dynamic zone, subject to a number of geomorphological processes. These are superimposed on a gradual uplift of the north of the country and a gradual subsidence of the south east due to adjustments following the retreat of ice sheets.

2.2.6 Approximately 7 per cent of the coastline is subject to erosion; 7 per cent is accreting and the remainder is stable. Along the sections of beaches and other unconsolidated shore lines the figures are 19 per cent, 24 per cent and 56 per cent respectively. Low lying coastal regions are liable to marine flooding at particularly high tides and during storm surges and it is estimated that about 1.5 million people are protected from such flooding in England and Wales.[32] Present flood risk areas can be plotted from surveys carried out by the then Water Authorities under Section 24(5) of the Water Act 1973, but unfortunately no single definition of 'flood risk' was used by the Authorities. Examples of criteria include the 1:100 year flood risk; areas below highest recorded tide and historic flood areas.[33] Some observers believe that a more accurate survey is still required as a basis for assessing future levels of flood risk.[34] However, a major survey of sea defences[35] is currently being undertaken by the National Rivers Authority (NRA), results of which will soon be available. Data include the condition of all existing defences and land at risk from flooding, defined (except for Anglian Region) with reference to the 1:200 year return period of still water level. Detailed maps are being produced with the aid of a Geographical Information System.[36]

Effects of sea level rise

2.2.7   Sea level rise in the UK is likely to result in increased erosion on some parts of the coast and an increase in the incidence of coastal flooding. For example, a 0.2m rise in mean sea level might in circumstances typical along parts of the south coast of England increase flood return periods from 100 years to five years.[37] However, the mean rise of sea level may be less important than the incidence of storms, which is impossible to predict with the current state of knowledge. A recent report on sea level rise in the UK emphasises this point:

'Unfortunately the lack of accurate data on the topography and the level of flood protection affored to low lying areas, and the uncertainties in the prediction of future storm conditions prevent quantitative statements on the changing coastal risk being made'.[38]

2.2.8   As noted in Section 1, the Climate Change Impacts Review Group (CCIRG) envisages global mean sea level rises of 20±10cms by 2030 and 30±15cms by 2050 (assuming a 'business as usual' emissions scenario). They suggest that these estimates are broadly applicable to the UK but must be adjusted for ongoing vertical land movements in specific coastal locations.

2.2.9   Sea level rise at the higher estimated levels would have significant implications for land resources and the built environment in some parts of the UK. Maps of land lying below the 5m and 10m contours have been plotted by the Ministry of Agriculture, Fisheries and Foods (MAFF), assuming that the land below 5m approximated to that afforded protection (contour lines below 5m do not exist on Ordnance Survey maps and therefore cannot be drawn on a national basis) and that the land between the 5m and 10m contours represents a 'buffer zone' (usualy quite narrow).[39] The summary

map (Figure 8) has been well-publicised, but is considered to be an inadequate basis for assessing future levels of flood risk.[40]

2.2.10   As noted above, it is difficult to make an accurate assessment of assets at risk from sea level rise. However, a detailed analyis of enhanced flood and erosion risk along the east coast from Hunstanton to Felixstowe has recently been carried out for the Ministry of Agriculture, Fisheries and Foods (MAFF) by the University of East Anglia (UEA). A similar study, for the south coast, is in progress at the University of Southampton.

2.2.11   In the UEA study, estimates at risk in the hazard zone (defined as inland to the 5m contour) were made for four sea level rise scenarios to 2050 (20cms, 40cms, 60cms and 80cms) and were then combined with three response scenarios (abandon, maintain or improve defences) in a partial cost benefit anaysis. The monetary value of assets was approximated by the amount of GDP potentially at risk in the hazard zone, expressed in present value terms. The effects of sea level rise on flood return curves was estimated by adding the potential rise to water levels of defined return periods and calculations of historic erosion rates and of the impact of sea level rise on the amount of retreat expected by 2050 were used to assess potential land losses under each scenario.[41] Net benefits of the two 'active' response strategies suggested that both would be economically viable on the basis of the restricted asset damage/ loss inventory (non-market losses or gains were not included); results are shown in Table 6. These results are heavily qualified by many uncertainties and simplifications.

2.2.12.   Since no allowance was made for adaptive responses in the flood hazard zone, the benefits of

Table 6   UEA Cost-Benefit Analysis: Present value of net benefits of 'active' response strategies* – flood and erosion hazard combined, 1990–2050

SLR Scenario (cms)	Response and flood type** scenario Net present benefits (£ million)			
	Maintain		Improve	
	A	B	A	B
20	972	966	1061	1058
40	943	933	1061	1058
60	938	926	1073	1071
80	904	885	1064	1063

Source: UEA Study, Executive Summary, p. 41.
* The present value of the **net benefit** of the two 'active' response strategies was computed by subtracting from the benefits (totals) the costs (capital plus maintenance) of the defence systems. Benefits were calculated in terms of the erosion/flood damage costs and losses avoided (i.e. in comparison with the do nothing abandon defence damage cost and loss burden).
** A assumes shallow and short duration flooding; B assumes deep and long duration.

Figure 8 Sea level rise: land potentially at risk from flooding

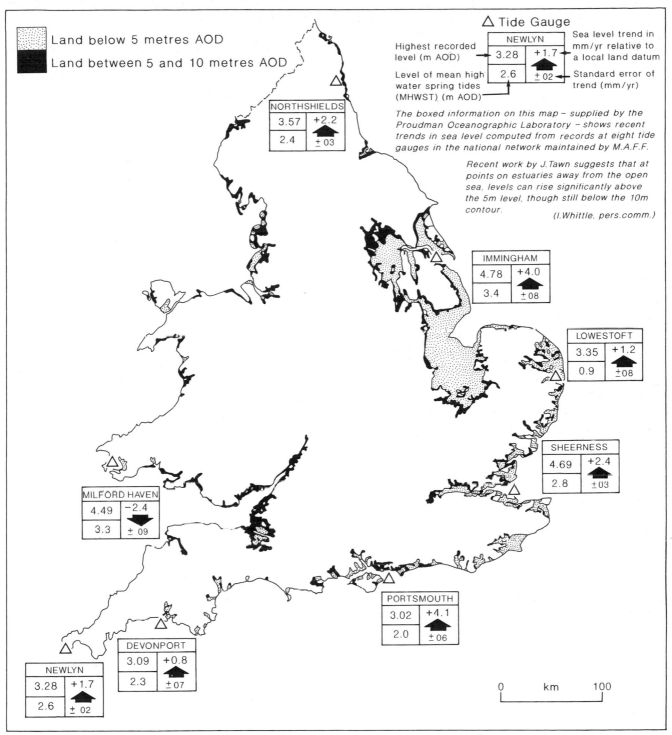

Source : Whittle 1990

protection may be overestimated. On the other hand, these benefits do not include protection of ecological or recreational assets. However, it is not clear whether protection of, for example, a coastal Site of Special Scientific Interest (SSSI) should always be considered a benefit. Some ecologists argue that in a holistic sense, nature conservation would benefit if society did not interfere with coastal dynamics: the resulting system would be different but possibly more 'valuable'.[42] Natural evolution of the coastline could be included as an option in cost benefit analysis, rather than assuming that protection of *existing* conservation interests would be a benefit, albeit one that is difficult to quantify.

27

Uncertainties

2.2.13 It is clear that considerable uncertainties remain. Predictions of global average sea level rise are themselves uncertain. These uncertainties increase substantially the greater the degree of spatial disaggregation. The frequency of extreme events, which may be of more importance than average sea levels for coastal dynamics, cannot be predicted meaningfully given the current state of knowledge. Even *existing* flood and erosion hazards are not adequately documented, nor is the full state of defences currently known. Finally, we cannot know how society will respond to the threat of sea level rise and the kinds of policies that will be adapted to deal with it in coastal zones. While sensitivity analysis would help, it would clearly become extremely complex in attempting to deal with all of these uncertainties.

2.2.14 The NRA has suggested that some of the major uncertainties about the impacts of sea level rise on UK coasts might be resolved in about 10 years. This seems optimistic, given the IPCC time scale for reducing major global uncertainties of at least 15 years and the additional problems arising from spatial disaggregation and prediction of extreme events.

Levels of response

2.2.15 In order to test the sensitivity of land use planning to possible responses to sea level rise we envisage three levels of policy response, as follows.

2.2.16 In a 'business as usual' scenario, existing coastal defence programmes are maintained, but no adjustment is made to allow for enhanced sea level rise due to climate change.

2.2.17 Sea defence policy already allows for some rise in sea level. Defences are renewed on rolling programme (approximately 5 years) and have theoretical lifetimes varying from 30 to 100 years, depending on nature of defence (whether hard or soft etc.). Complete renewal is unusual, but many of the defences constructed after the 1953 floods along the east coast will require repair or renewal in the fairly short term.

2.2.18 MAFF and the NRA have recently agreed to increase recommended allowances for rising sea level to 4–6mm per year, depending on the region (about 24–36cms by 2050).[43] If adopted, this might be sufficient to protect much of the coast from flooding for the next half century, if sea level rises in accordance with the central prediction (Figure 9).

Figure 9 Projected global mean sea level rise (cm) and design allowances

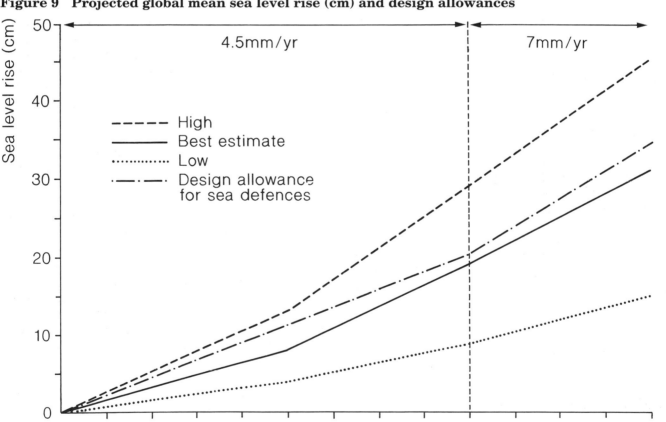

Note : Figure illustrates effect of increasing allowance after 2030

Source: I. Whittle, (NRA), 1991, pers. comm.

Under higher sea level rise scenarios, 'business as usual' would mean increased erosion and an increased risk of flood. Eventually, therefore, some land and infrastructure would have to be abandoned under this level of response.

2.2.19   The second level of response – 'status quo' – envisages political pressure being exerted successfully to maintain the existing level of *protection* of land and infrastructure. When sea level rises above a certain point it means improving the level of defence and in higher sea level rise scenarios might involve very considerable public expense.

2.2.20   If sea level rises in line with higher predictions, 'business as usual' and 'status quo' strategies may prove unacceptable on grounds of damage costs and protection costs respectively, though this is unlikely to become apparent for several decades. The alternative is an 'enhanced adaptive response' involving a combination of options identified by the IPCC Working Group III Coastal Zone Management Sub-Group.[44] Resources would be diverted to those areas where the most extensive and/or valuable assets are at risk, for example, densely populated areas, major communications links or industrial infrastructure; the highest quality agricultural land and some key Notified Nature Reserves might be included. In other areas, adaptive responses would be needed (such as revised building standards) or, where this is likely to be insufficient, planned retreat. Some parts of the coast would be allowed to evolve naturally. Land use planning would have a role in adaptation and planned retreat through development control. It is a feature of this scenario that there is greater co-ordination of coastal zone management, including land use planning.

2.2.21   We might extend this basic framework to include a 'do nothing' response, that is one in which even existing defences are not maintained. The UEA study included such an option as a base line against which to compare other policies. 'Do nothing' has some features in common with 'business as usual' (but the effects will be more extreme), and with enhanced adaptation where defences would be abandoned in some areas, though as part of a planned response. The other two UEA scenarios equate with our 'business as usual' and 'status quo' options. The UEA investigators did not consider policies of adaptation or selective retreat.

Lane use planning implications

2.2.22   The land use planning implications of sea level rise depend both on the rate of change in sea level and on the nature of the response adopted; these two factors are themselves clearly interrelated.

Existing defences, with the recently increased allowance for sea level rise, may provide an acceptable level of protection from flooding at least to 2030 if sea level rises according to central predictions, though the effects of waves and storms cannot be predicted at present. Higher rises would increase risks and/or costs of protection, but there is nevertheless likely to be a considerable period of time within which decisions about appropriate responses can be made. Allowances could be increased, if necessary, when current defences come to the end of their useful life (see Figure 9). Erosion analysis in the UEA study indicated that in areas where erosion rates of 1m/year are currently experienced, the shore line could have retreated inland by 58–400m by 2050, with a best estimate of just over 100m. Where erosion rates are low (0.1m/year), the best estimate suggests a retreat of around 10m by 2050.

Implications of loss of land and infrastructure

2.2.23   In the 'business as usual' and 'enhanced adaptive response' scenarios, damage to and ultimately losses of land and infrastructure would be sustained, especially if sea levels rise in accordance with the higher predictions. Effects would be similar, but more extreme, in a 'do nothing' scenario.

2.2.24   Where buildings and other infrastructure are lost, there will be a need for their relocation outside the flood or erosion hazard zone. Over time, and in the higher sea level rise scenarios, the land requirements for relocation could be considerable. Industrial installations are usually on the coast for a good reason, so it is unlikely that they would wish to relocate far inland. For housing, relocation requirements would be more flexible. The challenge to the land use planning system would be greater if the need for relocation became apparent very rapidly (for example, because of the occurrence of severe flooding with a very short return period).

2.2.25   Less direct implications for land use planning might arise if extensive areas of high quality agricultural land were lost. This may increase the priority to be afforded to agricultural land nationally and to some extent reverse the recent trend towards placing less emphasis on agricultural land in land use decisions (DoE Circular 16/87[45], for example, significantly reduces the requirement to consult MAFF over the development of agricultural land). This is a speculative impact and would depend on the overall context of agricultural policy and the perceived need for food production, matters which are currently in a state of flux.

Need for improved or new defences

2.2.26   New and improved defences feature in both the *'status quo'* and 'enhanced adaptive response' strategies (in selected areas in the latter case). They would have a potentially significant environmental impact and some works would be subject to environmental assessment.[46] New defence works require planning permission; in other cases the local planning authority is a statutory consultee.

2.2.27 Under higher sea level rise predictions there is likely to be increasing tension between pressures to maintain protection and the escalating cost of doing so. The adverse visual and environmental impacts of particular schemes would almost certainly be a factor in this conflict and is an area where local planning authorities are likely to become involved.

2.2.28 An indirect planning implication of this scenario arises from the materials requirements for improving defences, which could be considerable. Minerals extraction is already a contentious planning issue in the UK, especially in sensitive areas such as national parks, though the destination of the material has not been accepted by the Secretary of State for the Environment as a material consideration in planning decisions. CCIRG notes that coastal defences may require large stones and coastal quarries are usually used to meet such demands; boulders weighing up to five tonnes were needed for the repair of recent damage to coastal defences at Towyn in North Wales, and these are larger than usually quarried.[47]

2.2.29 Material for re-nourishing beaches may be dredged but this requires a licence. Under present restrictions on location of abstraction, material is costly and obtained in competition with the construction industry. These restrictions and the possible use of material unsuitable for building are under review.[48]

2.2.30 In the same way as materials requirements for flue gas desulphurisation have entered the debate about the merits of this approach to pollution abatement, so the indirect environmental costs of improving coastal defences might enter the calculus in the 'status quo' scenario.

The role of land use planning in adaptive response

2.2.31 The threat of sea level rise, whether or not it is realised, may act as a focus for a number of emerging themes in relation to coastal defence and management. It is already being used to support a growing body of opinion which questions the conventional wisdom of seeking to maintain the 'status quo' in coastal zones at whatever cost.[49] Pressures for more coordinated and longer-term coastal zone management are likely to grow and the implications for

land use planning are significant and merit more detailed analysis.

2.2.32 In a co-ordinated policy, development control would be an important part of a wider strategy for coastal zone management. Planning permission would not be granted in areas at risk from erosion and would be refused or made conditional upon specified building measures (such as floor heights) in flood hazard zones. The seaward extension of the remit of the land use planning system might also be considered. Land use planning would become an important means of internalising risk in flood hazard areas, itself a key part of an adaptive response. Such changes are an integral part of our 'enhanced adaptive response' strategy, but even in the 'business as usual' scenario, there is likely to be increasing pressure to enforce development control policies as increased flood and erosion hazards manifest themselves, so that the inventory of infrastructure at risk is not increased.

2.2.33 Currently, local planning authorities are required to consult the NRA about proposed development in flood risk areas and particularly to 'bear in mind' flood hazards.[50] Problems of coastal erosion are also recognised in planning policy guidance; PPG 14 states that:

'. . . coastal authorities may wish to consider the introduction of a presumption against built development in areas of coastal landslides or rapid coastal erosion. Consideration may also need to be given to the possible use of Article 4 Directions under the General Development Order 1988 in some circumstances to control permitted development. The fact that stabilisation works may, by their size and location, involve the need for environmental assessment may also need to be recognised in the criteria established in the Local Plan'.[51]

2.2.34 The basis for development control as part of an adaptive response therefore already exists, but to date controls have been relatively weak and there is a problem with the essentially retroactive nature of the consultation process.[52] More stringent policies are already implemented in a number of other countries (Figure 10). In areas not already developed, the 'coastal protection zone' could continue in low intensity agricultural use or could be available for amenity and conservation.

2.2.35 One of the first British structure plans to propose such policies is that of Norfolk. Policy FP 3 in the draft plan states that:

'There will be a presumption against development in areas likely to be affected by marine erosion within 75 years'.

Figure 10 Coastal zone set back policies in different countries

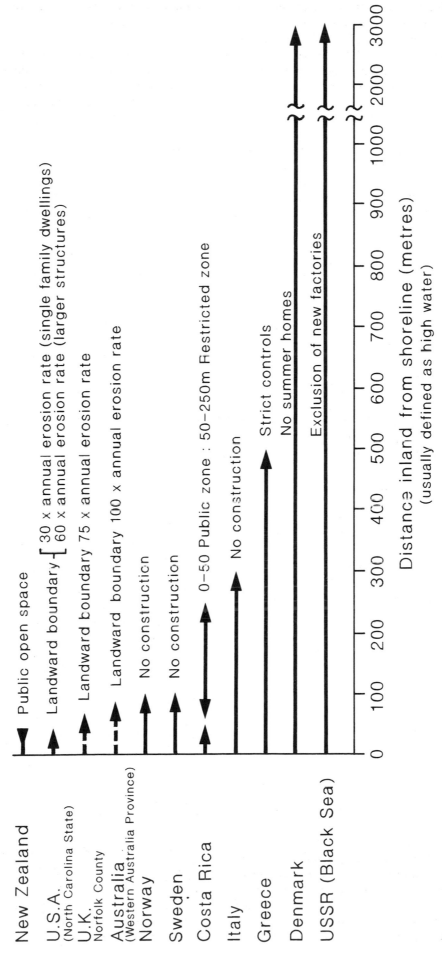

Source : Kay 1991

2.2.36 The possibility of a rising sea level is cited in the explanatory memorandum as justification for this 'variable definition setback' policy.[53]

2.2.37 In relation to flood risk, the draft Plan (Policy FP 2) states that:

'In areas liable to flood, or which would be affected by a major incursion by the sea, there will be a presumption against major development. Where development is permitted, minimum floor levels will be agreed with the National Rivers Authority'.[54]

2.2.38 Such a strategy would require delineation of areas where risk was sufficiently great to justify strict development control policies, and would therefore require the definition of 'acceptable risk'. A possible framework is provided by the 'standards of service' concept for sea defences, which involves classifying land use into a number of bands for which different standards of defence (defined, for example, in terms of flood return periods) might be appropriate (Table 7)[55]. This concept is being developed by the NRA, but minimum standards have not yet been endorsed.

2.2.39 Flood risk areas would also need to be defined with some accuracy: Kay identifies this as 'the biggest problem' facing local planning authorities seeking to implement such policies.[56] He suggests that special flood hazard maps will need to be drawn up by the NRA and that the Department of the Environment will need to provide scientific advice to guide the positioning of setback lines. Most importantly, he argues, the Department will need to provide 'the policy backing to uphold planning appeals'.[57]

2.2.40 Development control could reduce economic vulnerability in defined hazard zones over time, thereby reducing the present value of 'benefits' from

Table 7   Land use bands proposed for defining standards of service for sea defences

Land Use Band
Band A: containing urban elements over significant proportion of its length, or densely populated/developed over some of its length; amenity use may be prominent.
Band B: housing or non-residential property, less dense than Band A; possibly some intensive agriculture.
Band C: Isolated rural communities with residential/commercial interests; farming interests more apparent than for Bands A and B.
Band D: Isolated residential/commercial properties at risk from flooding; agricultural use, mainly arable, prominent; possible amenity interest.
Band E: Very few properties or roads. Agriculture, mainly grassland in floodplain. Limited amenity interests.

Source: See text

sea or coastal defences. (This effect is recognised in the UEA study, but not incorporated into the cost benefit analysis). However, development control itself incurs costs: it requires administration, imposes opportunity costs and, in the case of defining hazard zones, may result in devaluation of existing property. The lower the perceived risk, the less acceptable such costs are likely to be. Development control might also entail costs in terms of compensating existing property owners, though this is a contentious area and would require new legislation. Currently, there are institutional mechanisms to *stop* the coast retreating, but not to *allow* it to retreat while compensating those who might otherwise be protected.[58]

2.2.41 Currently twenty-eight different government departments or agencies manage the coastline to varying degrees.[59] The 'enhanced adaptive response' scenario would entail much greater co-ordination among these authorities. Co-ordination would enable coastal planning to be more holistic so that protection of one part of the coast did not starve another of material and lead to even greater demand for protection, and so that development was not simply permitted to take place incrementally in areas at risk up to the point where there is sufficient critical mass to exert pressure for protection, the cost of which would be met from the public purse.

2.2.42 The scenario would require better information than is currently available. For example, new maps need to be provided to local planning authorities to enable them to relate flood/erosion risk to development control policies. Currently there are no maps of erosion risk areas and maps of flood hazard zones are inadequate. Such information, together with policy guidance, could then provide a basis for appropriate planning policies. For example, a general policy statement on the account to be taken of physical constraints might be appropriate for the structure plan, while the local plan would set out in detail the criteria to be used in determining planning applications.[60] Information and new institutional arrangements both require time, but it is generally accepted that sea level rise is unlikely to present increased hazards in the short term.

Research needs

2.2.43 A number of empirical and theoretical research needs can be identified. Some concern the provision of information and the monitoring of current practice; others are concerned with frameworks for assessing the value of land use planning as part of an adaptive policy response.

- Better maps of hazard zones are required for use by local planning authorities.

- Since adaptive responses may require more stringent development control policies it would be valuable to identify the constraints which militate against better enforcement of *existing* policies, such as that relating to flood hazard zones.

- Further analyses of infrastructure at risk would be useful. This could be undertaken within a spatially-defined framework (considering all infrastructure at risk in defined areas), or a sectoral framework, assessing the risks to certain critical sectors, for example transport, on a national basis.

- There is a need to find ways of fitting land use planning, as an element of adaptive policy, into cost benefit frameworks such as that set out in the UEA study.

- Where uncertainty is a very signigicant feature of an issue, a decision analysis may provide a useful framework for policy choices and for determining the value of information. For illustration, a very simple framework, assuming either full development control or none, and a specified sea level rise or none is shown in Figure 11. Such a framework could be elaborated to include more factors and to allow for sensitivity analysis. For example, a range of possible sea level rises by particular dates and a range of possible development controls could be included. Existing and new assets could be differentiated and allowance made for other benefits, both of coastal protection (for example protecting recreational assets) and of development control. The probability that there would be investment in protection (for example, under political pressure in some of the 'branches' of the framework) could also be added. The framework could be used to assess the value of information. The utilities of the different outcomes need to be assessed, as do the probabilities of sea level rise occurring. Again, it would be possible to conduct a sensitivity analysis. Elaboration of the framework in this way would be a fairly major undertaking but it could be a worthwhile exercise.

- Some work is required on the possible costs of compensation. Revised policies might require compensation if planning permissions are revoked, or if the law is changed to permit existing property owners in hazard zones to be compensated if no further development is permitted and further defence work is limited. It would be particularly valuable to compare these costs with those of improving defences.

Summary

2.2.44 The likelihood of the different levels of response being adopted in the coastal zone depends in part on the magnitude and timing of sea level rise, the severity and frequency of floods and the incidence of erosion. 'Business as usual' is the most likely strategy in the short-medium term, merging into 'status quo' if the physical changes, as they manifest themselves and as predictions improve, seem manageable. 'Enhanced adaptive response' purely in anticipation of greenhouse-induced sea level rise seems unlikely except perhaps in the long term, but there are growing pressures anyway for integrated coastal zone management and sea level rise may be a vehicle to advance views that are already gaining ground. Because of the many actors involved and the many interests at stake from maintaining the 'status quo', comprehensive coastal zone management will be difficult to achieve. There may be partial implementation, however, for example through better development control.

2.2.45 Links with land use planning are potentially significant because of the impact of flood and erosion hazards on land resources and infrastructure, with possible requirements for relocation; because sea and coastal defences have significant enrivonmental impacts (aesthetic and in broader terms, for example on other coastal areas and for materials); and, most importantly, because land use planning would be a key instrument of integrated coastal zone management which could provide the best framework for enhanced adaptation should it become necessary.

2.2.46 Greater certainty about physical impacts is unlikely to be forthcoming for at least 10–15 years. Existing defences are renewed on a rolling programme (approximately 5 years) and have theoretical lifetimes varying from 30–100 years. Many of the east coast defences constructed after the 1953 floods

Figure 11 Decision analysis framework

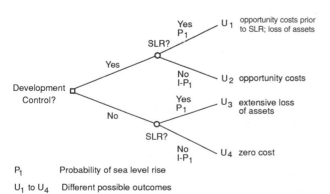

P_1 Probability of sea level rise

U_1 to U_4 Different possible outcomes

will require repair or renewal in the short term. In most cases, the relevant decision is whether to renew or not: extra height to allow for sea level rise is unlikely to add greatly to costs. Existing allowances, if implemented, are likely to provide adequate protection until well into the next century. There is probably a period of at least two decades in which to gather more information and formulate policies.

2.2.47   Research needs focus on better information, particularly maps of hazard zones, to enable local planning authorities to play a role in hazard management and identification of the constraints which militate against better enforcement of *existing* policies, such as that relating to flood hazard zones; further analyses of infrastructure at risk from sea level rise; and the development of frameworks to evaluate land use planning as an element of adaptive policy, including cost benefit analysis and decision analysis.

2.3 TRANSPORT

Climate change, transport and land use planning

2.3.1 Responses in the transport sector to the threat of climate change are potentially among the most important for land use planning. Because of the complexities involved they are also among the most difficult to assess. In this Chapter we consider the current situation and options for reducing emissions of rfgs, outline three possible levels of policy response and explore the implications for land use planning.

2.3.2 The transport sector accounts for an increasing proportion of final energy demand in the UK.[61] It produces about 22 per cent of total UK carbon dioxide emissions, as well as substantial proportions of total emissions of other gases with a greenhouse effect, including oxides of nitrogen (NO_x) (45 per cent), hydrocarbons (28 per cent) and carbon monoxide (85 per cent).[62] These contributions are growing: for example, carbon dioxide emissions from road vehicles rose by 27 per cent between 1978 and 1987, while emissions from all ground based sources fell by 5 per cent.[63] By 2005, the year in which overall carbon dioxide emissions are intended to be stabilised at their 1990 levels, car mileage is predicted to increase by between 31 and 52 per cent.[64]

2.3.3 Traffic growth reflects land use and transport trends which have reinforced each other over several decades to produce an increasingly mobile society. Decentralisation of population and employment to the suburbs and, since the 1950s, to smaller free-standing settlements in non-metropolitan areas, has been permitted by rapidly increasing personal mobility. One consequence, with major implications for travel patterns, has been the increasing physical separation of homes, jobs and other facilities, reinforced by the concentration of shops, schools, hospitals and other services into fewer, larger units.

2.3.4 Lifestyles and trip patterns have become more complex and car-oriented[65] and the evolving distribution of land uses is increasingly difficult to serve by public or non-motorised transport. For example, decentralisation of population and employment has been associated with a significant increase in the amount of commuting and trips have become less focussed on central areas. In the South East, typical journeys to work are 40 per cent longer than they were twenty years ago.[66] But at the same time, the significance of the journey to work has diminished (now representing only 20 per cent of all trips[67]). Journeys for leisure, social activities and shopping have become more frequent and longer: for example, the number of shopping trips per week doubled in the period 1965–1985, with a significant increase in use of the car for this purpose.[68]

2.3.5 These trends, and parallel changes in freight transport, are well documented elsewhere[69], and are broadly expected to continue.[70] Road traffic forecasts produced in 1989 indicate that total traffic could increase by between 83 per cent and 142 per cent by the year 2025.[71] Though it is accepted that traffic growth on this scale cannot be accommodated[72], such forecasts indicate the magnitude of the task of controlling rfg emissions from the transport sector.

Relevance for land use planning

2.3.6 Because of the important interactions between land use and transport, many policies aimed at reducing the environmental impact of transport have implications for land use planning. Transport accounts directly for up to 20 per cent of land use in urban areas.[73] The availability and cost of transport are important factors in the evolution of land use; and land use patterns are key determinants of the demand for movement. Policies affecting the amount and mode of travel are likely to interact with locational trends in complex ways. They may also demand the proactive involvement of the land use planning system. These implications are considered in detail below.

Potential to reduce emissions of radiative forcing gases from the transport sector

2.3.7 Options for reducing emissions of rfgs from the transport sector include more economical driving, improving the energy efficiency of, and reducing emissions from, individual vehicles ('technical fix'), shifting to more energy-efficient modes and reducing the need to travel. The traditional policy instruments have been public investment, direct regulation and to some extent the provision of information. However, there is growing interest in the use of the price mechanism, including taxes or charges on fuel, vehicles or roads.

2.3.8 'Technical fix' options include pollution controls, improvements in energy efficiency and alternative fuels (such as methanol, natural gas, hydrogen or electricity[74]). The potential of such options to reduce emissions from the transport sector has been extensively reviewed elsewhere.[75] As with changes in driver behaviour, they do not impinge directly on land use planning, but two points are important in the present context.

2.3.9 First, in the absence of additional policy measures, many technical improvements are likely to be outweighed by the growth of traffic and by other factors such as a preference for larger and more powerful cars. For example, while energy efficiency is projected to improve by a maximum of 28 per cent by 2010[76], the 'low' forecast for vehicle kilometres projects an increase of 41 per cent.[77] Similarly, while European Community legislation requiring all cars to be fitted with catalytic converters will help reduce emissions of nitrogen oxides, hydrocarbons and carbon monoxide in the short term, these are likely to start to rise again early in the next century if traffic increases in line with government forecasts.[78] The second point is that other measures may be necessary if the benefits of 'technical fix' options are to be realised (for example, whatever their potential, cars will not run at maximum efficiency in congested conditions). If 'technical fix' measures prove insufficient to achieve emissions reduction targets, other policy options may be invoked.

2.3.10 We focus here on two broad policy options – inter-modal shift and reducing the need to travel – and on two sets of policy instruments – traffic management and fiscal measures – because these would seem to be the elements of a possible future transport policy having the strongest interaction with land use. We also consider the potential of the land use planning system itself as a policy instrument.

Inter-modal shift

2.3.11 Rail and bus systems are generally more energy-efficient than cars, but actual energy efficiencies are affected by a number of variables, including load factors. On the basis of average passenger loads, most estimates suggest that cars (and taxis) in urban areas use the most energy per passenger-kilometre, and buses (or minibuses) travelling in uncongested road conditions use the least; rail systems occupy a position somewhere in between (Figure 12).[79] The higher the load factor for public transport, the more significant its energy advantages become. Potential energy savings and carbon dioxide emissions reductions from inter-modal shift are difficult to quantify because of the large variability, but some estimates are shown in Table 8.

2.3.12 Because the private car is currently so dominant, even small shifts away from it imply large increases in demand for other forms of transport. A 5% shift from car to bus and rail would result in a 63 per cent increase in rail and bus demand.[80] Capacity constraints therefore represent an obstacle to modal shift, particularly for rail systems, in the short term.[81] Inter-modal shift from car to bus would be

Table 8 Estimates of energy savings and carbon dioxide emission reductions from modal shift

Author(s)	Form of shift: assumptions and energy savings	Energy saving/ carbon dioxide emission reduction
Maltby et al[1]	transfer of 50% of urban work trips by private vehicles to bus services	8–12% (energy)
ETSU[2]	10% transfer from car to public bus services	5% (energy)
ERRL/WWF[3]	Number of passengers on buses and trains doubles 1990–2005	15% (carbon dioxide)
Hughes and Potter[4]	Car use reduced by 5–10%	5–6% short term 12% long term (carbon dioxide)

1. Maltby et al (1978)
2. ETSU (1989)
3. ERRL (1989)
4. Hughes, P. and Potter, S. (1989) *Routes to Stable Prosperity* Milton Keynes, Energy and Environment Research Unit.

Figure 12 Primary energy requirements of different modes of transport

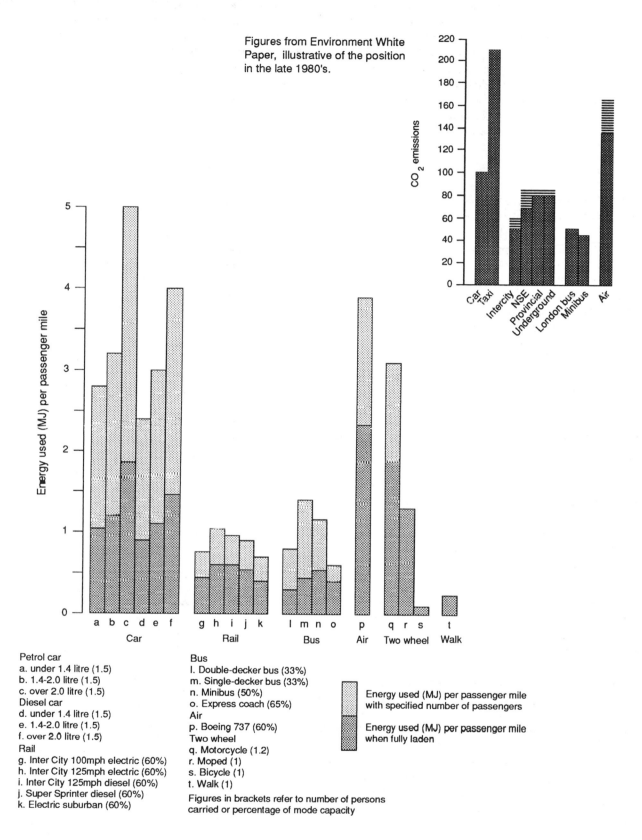

Figures from Environment White Paper, illustrative of the position in the late 1980's.

Petrol car
a. under 1.4 litre (1.5)
b. 1.4-2.0 litre (1.5)
c. over 2.0 litre (1.5)
Diesel car
d. under 1.4 litre (1.5)
e. 1.4-2.0 litre (1.5)
f. over 2.0 litre (1.5)
Rail
g. Inter City 100mph electric (60%)
h. Inter City 125mph electric (60%)
i. Inter City 125mph diesel (60%)
j. Super Sprinter diesel (60%)
k. Electric suburban (60%)

Bus
l. Double-decker bus (33%)
m. Single-decker bus (33%)
n. Minibus (50%)
o. Express coach (65%)
Air
p. Boeing 737 (60%)
Two wheel
q. Motorcycle (1.2)
r. Moped (1)
s. Bicycle (1)
t. Walk (1)

Figures in brackets refer to number of persons
carried or percentage of mode capacity

Energy used (MJ) per passenger mile
with specified number of passengers

Energy used (MJ) per passenger mile
when fully laden

Source (main figure) : Owens, S.E. (1991) *Energy-Conscious Planning*, London, CPRE, from Potter, S. and Hughes, P. (1990) *Vital Transport Statistics*, London, Transport 2000 table reproduced in Ryden, D. (1990) Energy use in Transport - Implications for Local Authority Policy (Draft), University of Exeter, Energy studies Unit.

cheaper and quicker to implement, but requires traffic management and dedicated road space if journey times are not to be unacceptably slow. Investment in new capacity has implications for land use planning which are considered in more detail below.

2.3.13 The present nature of freight operations constrains how much modal transfer is possible. Despite the potential of some technological developments such as 'piggy-backing', The Energy Technology Support Unit suggest that:

> 'The scope for modal transfers from road to rail would seem to be limited having regard to the characteristics of road freight, the relative economics of road and rail operations, the persistent distribution of industrial locations and the factors which influence freight users to decide on the best mode of transport for their requirements. Any such transfers would appear to offer only marginal fuel consumption benefits because the journey involving only road transport is often shorter than the one involving road transport at each end of a rail journey.'[82]

2.3.14 Nevertheless, such modal shift was a key objective of the recently announced initiatives in transport policy which include a tripling of the grant available towards the cost of freight facilities when there are 'worthwhile environmental benefits'.[83] Completion of the Channel Tunnel will provide new opportunities for rail freight and the potential for inter-modal freight systems (combined transport) is being explored.

Reducing the need to travel

2.3.15 There has been much recent discussion of the potential to reduce the *need* to travel. This might be achieved in two ways: by substituting telecommunications for travel, and by reducing the number and length of trips through appropriate location of different land uses. The latter has clear implications for land use planning, discussed in detail below.

TELECOMMUNICATIONS

2.3.16 It is often suggested that telecommunications will reduce the need for personal travel. Evidence for this substitution is currently slim. (Indeed, in some circumstances telecommunications may stimulate rather than replace travel, by establishing contacts who then need to meet). It is plausible that more people may be able to work from home for at least part of the time, and some organisations are already encouraging their employees to do this. However, the option is restricted, at least initially, to a relatively small group of professionals.

2.3.17 In the short term, developments in telecommunications seem unlikely to have a major impact on travel, though one estimate suggests that 17 per cent of the workforce might be working from home by 1995.[84] In the longer term, telecommuting and teleshopping, and perhaps telecommunications with doctors and various advisory services, may become significant, even if the effect is mainly to spread the travel peak. A comparison by British Telecom of the energy consumption for telephone calls and for travel (Table 9) suggests that energy savings and rfg emission reductions could be substantial. If a third of journeys were replaced by telecommuting for 4 million UK residents per year, about 8800 GWh per annum (2 per cent of present car energy use) could be saved.[85]

2.3.18 The effects of substituting telecommunications for travel could have significant implications for land use planning and are certainly too important to be ignored. As yet, however, the magnitude of any effect is unclear, and the relevant time scales are probably quite long. This is an area which we do not pursue in more detail here, but it is one whose implications should clearly be kept under review.

LAND USE PLANNING

2.3.19 Potential reductions in travel and energy demand from modification of land use patterns would also be long term and the effects cannot easily be isolated from those of other policies. However, a number of estimates have been made and in theory potential savings compare well with those which might be achieved by more conventional energy-efficiency measures. Transport energy demand varies by a factor of two or three between the most and least efficient land use patterns (Table 10).

2.3.20 Real savings would be less than maximum potential, because change is incremental, energy demand may not be as elastic as the models assume,

Table 9 Comparison of primary energy consumption for telephone calls and travel

Destination	Distance (km)	Primary energy for 30 min telephone call (MJ)	Primary operating energy for single person making return journey (MJ)
London	10	1.45	10 (double decker bus) 60 (car, 1.4–2.0 litres)
Manchester	320	5.82	1930 (car, 1.4–2.0 litres) 380 (rail, Intercity 125)
New York	5000	8.76 (submarine) 22.3 (satellite)	24400 (air, Boeing 737)

Source: British Telecom, summarised in Tuppen, C. (1991) 'Energy and telecommunications – an environmental appraisal', *UKCEED Bulletin*, 34, July–August, 12–14. Original data for travel figures from Hughes 1991.

Table 10 Influence of land use patterns on energy demand for transport

Land use variables	Mechanism	Energy implications
Combination of land use factors (shape, size, interspersion of land uses etc.)	travel requirements (esp. trip length and frequency)	variation of up to 150 per cent
Interspersion of activities	travel requirements (esp. trip length)	variation of up to 130 per cent
shape of urban area	travel requirements	variation of up to 20 per cent
density/clustering of trip ends	facilitates economic public transport	energy savings of up to 20 per cent

Source: Adapted from Owens, S. E. (1986) *Energy, Planning and Urban Form*, London, Pion. Figures come from a wide variety of sources in the literature.

the starting point may not be the worst case, and the optimum structure is unlikely to be achieved. On the other hand if modification of land use patterns were part of a more comprehensive policy package, different measures may reinforce each other to achieve even greater energy savings.

Traffic management

2.3.21 Traffic management, including control of traffic flow and speed, access and parking has considerable potential to improve energy efficiency and reduce pollution from vehicles. Much of the benefit comes from improved vehicle performance in less congested conditions. In the US, for example, studies of reversible lane systems have shown savings in trip times of up to 25 per cent, and fuel savings of 10 per cent[86]; traffic signal systems can deliver energy savings of three to 30 per cent, depending on time of day and other factors. Such savings may be offset if improvements in traffic flow release previously suppressed demand in congested areas.[87]

2.3.22 Traffic management can also encourage inter-modal shift, since some measures change the relative attractiveness of travel by different modes. These include dedicated bus lanes and deterrence of car use through parking and prohibition policies (some of these measures merge into fiscal policies which are discussed in more detail below). However, unless extended over a large enough area and combined with active support for public transport, car restraint policies in isolation may result in increased journey lengths and times rather than inter-modal shift, and the overall impact on energy efficiency may be negligible or even negative. They may also lead to development pressures outside the controlled zone.

Fiscal policies

2.3.23 There has been increasing interest in the use of the price mechanism as a transport policy instru-

ment, particularly for restraint of the private car. If fiscal measures influence travel behaviour, they may also have implications for land use planning.

2.3.24 The simplest option, and the one most closely related to energy demand and carbon dioxide and other emissions, would be to increase the already substantial tax on fuel. Evidence suggests that demand is relatively inelastic, with short-term elasticities of around −0.25 (for petrol).[88] A 20 per cent increase in petrol prices might therefore lead to a five per cent reduction in demand, mainly through marginal adjustment of trip patterns, especially social and leisure trips.[89] Evidence that people adopt such strategies is provided by surveys conducted in the aftermath of the fuel crisis of the early 1970s.[90]

2.3.25 Analysis of longer term response is problematic for a number of reasons, including the lack of a long period of sustained fuel price increases. Most lagged time series analyses show higher medium to long term than short term elasticities of demand for petrol. However, elasticities of demand for *travel* appear to diverge from those for fuel in the medium term; people find ways of saving fuel without loss of mobility (for example, by buying more efficient cars) and revert to their former trip patterns.[91] This suggests that the medium term response to fuel price increases would not have a major impact on travel patterns. In the long term elasticities of demand for *travel* might rise again as people adjust location and lifestyles, possibly at times of 'life shock', such as important transitions between life cycle stages. (Figure 13). There is some support for this hypothesis, though it currently amounts to little more than informed speculation and it is difficult to see how the major unknowns could satisfactorily be resolved.[92]

2.3.26 Road pricing is an alternative, or additional, fiscal instrument. Various options are, or soon will be available, of which the most sophisticated is elec-

Figure 13 Possible trends in traffic and petrol price elasticities over time

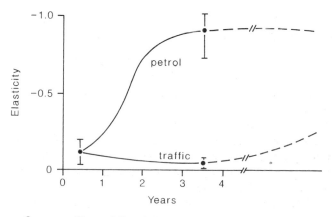

Source : Dix and Goodwin 1982

39

tronic road pricing. The basic concept is to charge motorists for their use of roads, and it is possible to have spatial and temporal variation of charges. In Singapore, an Area Licencing scheme resulted in an initial reduction in morning peak traffic of 70 per cent, settling down later to 22 per cent.[93] An analysis of possible ERP schemes for Hong Kong predicted reductions in peak time car traffic of 20–24 per cent. It also suggested that about 40 per cent of car trips would be unaffected (taking place outside the time or zone of charging), about 40 per cent of drivers would 'stay and pay', nine per cent would change their mode of travel and five per cent would change their time of travel. Fuel consumption would be reduced by 6–9 per cent; carbon monoxide emission by 14–17 per cent, nitrogen oxide emissions by about 6 per cent and emission of hydrocarbons by about 3 per cent.[94] A study of cordon charges in Central London suggested that with a charge (in 1989) of £3 per day, weekday traffic with a Central London destination would be reduced by 30 per cent, and that demand for buses would increase by 15 per cent and for trains/ tubes by 7 per cent.[95] There is some evidence, then, that road pricing would encourage inter-modal shift. Longer term impacts on locational behaviour do not seem to have been considered.

2.3.27 For fiscal policies to be effective the price message must reach car drivers. It is generally accepted, therefore, that fiscal restraint would have to include continued reduction of the tax advantages of company cars so that all but essential users would actually become exposed to price messages.

Levels of policy response

2.3.28 We have considered three levels of policy response in the transport sector to the threat of climate change. These are not quantified scenarios, but have provided a way of structuring the analysis of potential land use planning implications.

2.3.29 The 'business as usual' response is essentially a continuation of current policies[96] with no measures other than those already agreed to reduce rfg emissions from the transport sector. The existing road building programme[97] would proceed and, in line with current trends and commitments, certain traffic management schemes and initiatives to encourage freight transport by rail would be implemented. There would be modest investment in public transport (from both public and private sources). For example, the planned investment in the London Underground would be undertaken and a handful of the 37 light rapid transit (LRT) schemes currently at the planning stage[98] might be financed. It is explicitly not government policy to cater for all fore-cast demand[99], but significant policy restraint on road traffic is not a feature of this scenario.

2.3.30 A second level of response, essentially a 'no regrets' scenario, involves transport policies which result in rfg emissions abatement but which are implemented because they deliver other net benefits. For example, there might be greater emphasis on reducing congestion for economic reasons, with more radical traffic management schemes, including park and ride facilities and greater control over parking in central urban areas (envisaged as a possibility in the Environment White Paper[100]). This could involve a higher level of capital funding of urban public transport by Central Government, and therefore more investment in LRT. Fiscal measures in this scenario would aim to make the market more transparent. For example, road pricing schemes would be implemented on a limited basis in central areas of some of the most congested cities, the burden of taxation would continue gradually to shift from vehicle excise duty to fuel, and tax differentiation might be used to discriminate between more and less efficient vehicles at the point of sale.

2.3.31 We envisage a third level of response – the 'enhanced emissions reduction' scenario – in which the transport sector would bear a greater share of the pollution abatement required to meet increasingly stringent targets. Ceilings would be set on emissions by particular dates which would require a reduction in the rate of growth of traffic. A model is provided by the Netherlands *National Environmental Policy Plan* which sets upper limits on emissions of NO_x, hydrocarbons and carbon dioxide from the transport sector for the years 2000 and 2010. It seeks to limit the growth of traffic to 30 per cent and 35 per cent respectively by these dates, to double the use of public transport and to achieve a modal shift to bicycles for journeys of 5–10 kilometres.[101] The option of tightening these targets is kept open.

2.3.32 In this scenario the object would be to reduce carbon dioxide emissions from the transport sector by at least 20 per cent by the year 2010. A wide range of policy instruments would be employed, including traffic management and restraint, discrimination in favour of walking and cycling, substantially increased investment in public transport, fiscal measures including fuel tax and road pricing and land use planning measures to reduce journey distances and to encourage the use of public transport. We envisage use of excise duties to increase the real price of fuel annually in real terms and implementation of road pricing schemes in most major towns and cities. There would be significant investment in public transport with LRT schemes being widely adopted.

Land use planning implications

2.3.33 The main areas of interaction between policies in the transport sector and land use planning may be summarised as follows:

- certain traffic management schemes have a land use dimension;

- inter-modal shift may involve land take for infrastructure;

- traffic restraint and/or more investment in public transport may lead in the longer term to redistribution of development pressures; and

- land use planning itself may be employed as a policy instrument to influence modal choice or to reduce the need for movement.

2.3.34 We consider each of these interactions in turn, with reference to the three levels of response outlined above.

Traffic management

2.3.35 Traffic management will be implemented with increasing vigour from the 'business as usual' to the 'enhanced emissions reduction' level of response.

2.3.36 Many measures to control the flow and speed of traffic have few direct implications for land use planning, though traffic control may be an important feature of more comprehensive urban policies such as area improvement schemes, which may require active co-operation between transport and planning authorities. Some measures, for example pedestrianisation and 'red routes', will affect the character and function of the areas in which they are imposed and will therefore be of relevance in the formulation of local planning policies.

2.3.37 Parking restrictions may require the involvement of local planning authorities especially where they are strictly imposed and extended to cover private parking spaces, as we might envisage in the 'enhanced emissions reduction' scenario. The co-ordinated policy required by this level of response would entail careful control over the provision of parking spaces in new development and a revision of current planning practice. (The Environment White Paper suggests that 'provision for car parking for employees should take account of the availability of other means of transport'.[102] There is already some guidance to local planning authorities on this issue, but restrictions are difficult to enforce and we consider that this would continue to be the case in the 'business as usual' and 'no regrets' scenarios).

2.3.38 Generally the land use planning implications of traffic management schemes are relatively minor; many are already familiar and introduce few novel issues.

Inter-modal shift: infrastructure requirements

2.3.39 Provision of better facilities for cyclists and pedestrians will have implications for land use planning at the local scale. In the Netherlands 'extra infrastructural measures' are envisaged to encourage bicycle use, including 'bicycle routes in and around the towns, notably in commuter corridors, routes to and from stations and bicycle parking facilities'.[103] Development of extensive cycle routes in the UK is likely to involve co-operation between neighbouring local authorities, and provision for parking of bicycles might become a condition of planning consent. Careful planning will be required to minimise conflict between pedestrians and cyclists. All of these are primarily transport planning matters, but they have a land use dimension and the need for active co-operation between those involved in land use and transport planning is likely to be more strongly felt as the emphasis on non-motorised transport increases. Much could be learnt from those local authorities in Britain which have pioneered the provision of cycle routes, and from the Netherlands, where a policy of motorised and non-motorised traffic segregation is pursued.

2.3.40 In a similar way, discrimination in favour of buses, for example through the use of bus lanes, has a land use dimension. More significant may be the need to provide interchange facilities to permit the better integration of different forms of transport (for example, bus/rail interchange or park and ride schemes), and to identify routes for light rail systems. There are physical implications for local plans as well as procedural implications relating to the need for integration of the land use and transport planning processes at this level. There is likely to be some degree of controversy, for example, over the provision of light rail routes and edge-of-town car parks, and there are potential implications for green belt policy. These needs, and their implications for land use planning, increase through the three levels of response with the degree of emphasis on public transport. They are small in the 'business as usual' scenario, but in an 'enhanced emissions reduction' strategy modal shift would be encouraged by a combination of regulatory and fiscal incentives as well as new investment, and requirements for new facilities would be therefore be extensive.

2.3.41 Although even a modest shift from road to rail, such as might be envisaged in the 'no regrets' scenario, would result in a substantial increase in demand for rail, increased patronage in all levels of response could largely be accommodated by increasing the capacity of existing lines. In any case, as selection of a rail route to the Channel Tunnel has demonstrated, land use and environmental implications represent a real constraint on the planning of such routes. New stations are likely to be needed however in the 'enhanced emissions reduction' scenario and to some extent in 'no regrets'. Kent's transport strategy, for example, notes that potential exists for encouraging greater use of local rail services for work and shopping, but that this would require the provision of additional stations and higher frequency services.[104] This clearly has land use implications.

2.3.42   In general, the infrastructure, land use and planning implications of varying degrees of inter-modal shift merit more detailed consideration.

Redistribution of development pressures

2.3.43   Transport links are a key influence on land development pressures. Changes in the availability and cost of transport which might induce inter-modal shift or reduce the demand for movement might therefore be reflected in a redistribution of such pressures. It is not possible, given the many uncertainties and the relatively long time scales involved, to predict the nature of this redistribution with confidence. Some indication can be gleaned from the use of urban models, but there are many qualifications which need to be taken into account.

2.3.44   Restraint of the private car and the provision of new public transport facilities could lead directly to new development pressures. For example, parking restrictions in central areas, especially if extended to private parking spaces, will increase the attraction of out-of-town locations for employment and services.[105] This phenomenon is already apparent, mainly as a result of congestion, but it illustrates what might happen if regulatory restrictions are not supported by fiscal measures. If travel is cheap but central areas are unfriendly to cars, development pressures will inevitably arise elsewhere. In other words, the 'give' is in land use not mode of travel. Similarly, the association of development pressures with transport nodes is well established and is likely to be a feature of, for example, new rail and light rail stations. (Encouragement of such development as a planning policy is considered below.)

2.3.45   In a much more general sense, restraints on travel are likely to lead to modifications to land use patterns, just as increasing mobility has had a profound influence on patterns of development to date. These effects are, however, very difficult to predict. A fundamental problem lies in our lack of understanding of the response to increased costs of travel (in terms of time and/or money). People and firms may

respond to such constraints in a number of ways but it is only if they modify their travel behaviour that there is likely to be a longer-term influence on land use. We have already considered the evidence which suggests that price elasticities of demand for fuel and demand for travel must be considered separately and have shown that it cannot be assumed that people will travel less (after some initial adjustments) in the face of constraints on private transport. The cross elasticities of demand for different forms of transport are also important in this context. There is evidence that the frequency and reliability of public transport are more significant factors in modal shift than price.[106]

2.3.46   Nevertheless, it remains a plausible hypothesis that individuals might adjust their travel habits in the longer term by relocation or changes in behaviour which, in aggregate, would influence residential location and the locational decisions of employers and service providers. The important question then becomes how land use patterns might adjust and this issue has been quite extensively explored with the aid of urban models.

2.3.47   Increasing the significance of travel costs in urban models almost invariably leads to less travel and the closer integration of different activities, such as residential areas and employment centres. This has been demonstrated with Lowry-type models, utility analyses and with methods from dynamical systems theory.[107] However, the use of models in a predictive capacity is subject to serious limitations. For example, the values assigned to model variables must either be measured empirically or assumed subjectively, involving problems of uncertainty and simplification.[108] Critics argue that results of these exercises are not surprising given the assumptions built into the models, and question whether the effect of a change in transport costs can in fact be accurately modelled.[109]

2.3.48   If we accept these quite serious limitations, however, the models suggest some reversal of the trend towards increasing separation of activities, but not necessarily a reversal of the trend towards decentralisation. The outcome might be a pattern of 'decentralised concentration', with existing urban and suburban centres becoming increasingly attractive. Travel restraint superimposed on the process of decentralisation from the major metropolitan areas might lead to the greatest development pressures in urban and suburban centres with a good mix of facilities, a high quality of life and perhaps also good longer-distance travel links. Locations accessible only by road, such as the periphery of the larger cities and green field sites in rural areas, might become less attractive for many activities.

2.3.49 These possibilities are too speculative to justify any specific planning system response. But in any case, it is unlikely that such changes would take place independently of the land use planning system. In any scenario in which travel restraints are great enough to have a longer-term impact on development pressures, the land use planning system is itself likely to be a policy instrument in reducing the demand for travel.

Land use planning as a policy instrument

2.3.50 The most significant implications for land use planning in relation to the transport sector will arise if land use planning itself becomes an instrument to bring about changes in travel patterns. Forward planning and development control would seek to encourage land use patterns that reduce the need to travel or encourage the use of energy-efficient modes. There are major implications for land use planning at all scales. Appropriate policies would need to be adopted in structure plans, local plans and unitary development plans, and enforced through development control. It is likely that legislation or at least policy guidance would be required and planning education would need to take this issue on board. Research on energy-efficient land use patterns gives some indication of the types of policies that might be required.

2.3.51 At the urban and regional scales, the single most important factor affecting travel needs is the physical separation of activities. The key variables in this relationship are density and the degree of mixing of different land uses. Theoretical work shows fairly unambiguously that as urban density increases, energy use for transport falls.[110] In the real world, as always, the relationship is less clear, but the theoretical predictions are broadly confirmed by cross-sectional studies and analysis of travel patterns within large metropolitan areas (Figure 14 and Table 11).[111]

2.3.52 Policies to reduce travel needs might aim to bring homes, jobs and services together in a relatively compact urban centre to achieve a high level of assessibility with little need for movement. Many studies suggest that concentration of development is an energy-efficient form[112], and it is a development pattern strongly endorsed by the European Commission in its recent *Green Paper on the Urban Environment*.[113] Centralisation also has certain disadvantages, including congestion and other disamenities, and gives rise to concern about 'town cramming'. One important factor here, however, is the large amount of land demanded by the private car in urban areas. A Norwegian study currently in progress suggests that if dependence on the car could be reduced, considerable amounts of land might be

Table 11   Residential densities, automobile ownership and use, and transit use, Greater Toronto Area (Fall, 1986)

	Core	Inner Suburbs	Outer Suburbs
Population	910,400	1,224,300	1,504,500
Persons per square Km	**5,300**	**2,780**	**1,440**
Vehicles per 1,000 persons	407	526	572
Households with no vehicle	30%	15%	1%
Households with >1 vehicle	21%	40%	64%
Total daily trips per person	1.95	2.13	2.28
Trips made by automobile	55%	70%	81%
Trips made by transit	32%	33%	9%
Trips made by bicycling or walking	13%	8%	10%
Average trip length by auto (km)	8.7	9.0	11.8
Average trip length by transit (km)	6.1	9.1	13.3
Km/day/person by automobile	9.4	13.4	21.7
Km/day/person by transit	3.8	4.2	2.8
Grams of CO_2/person/day*	**2,100**	**2,940**	**4,520**
Tonnes of CO_2/person/year	**0.77**	**1.07**	**1.65**

* Assumes 200 grams of CO_2 emitted per person-kilometre by automobile and 60 grams per person-kilometre by public transit.

Source: Gilbert (1991) *Cities and Global Warming*, Toronto, Canadian Urban Institute.

released, minimising potential conflicts between the need for urban green space and a more compact pattern of urban development.[114]

2.3.53 An alternative strategy would be to decentralise some jobs and services and relate them to residential areas, either *within* a single large urban area, or to form freestanding settlements which may or may not retain links with the original centre. Many studies have found 'decentralised concentration' to be relatively efficient in terms of travel and energy requirements.[115]

2.3.54 However, there are major uncertainties about the potential energy advantages of decentralised mixed development. Reducing travel requirements may incur costs in terms of amenity or access to a range of jobs and services: what matters is how individuals trade off these different costs against each other. When alternative development patterns are modelled and ranked according to energy efficiency, the results are sensitive to assumptions about future lifestyles and the way in which people value mobility and choice. If rising energy costs or policy restraints restrict mobility, a pattern of 'decentralised concentration' may be energy efficient because people will tend to use the jobs and services which are close to them. But if travel costs pose only a minimum deterrent, such a pattern may be more

Figure 14   Gasoline use per capita versus population density, 1980

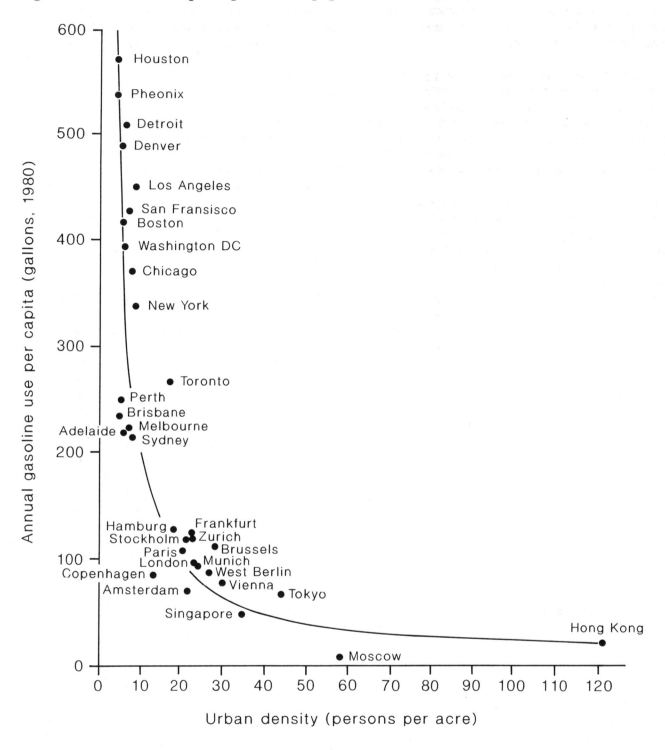

Source : Newman and Kenworthy 1989

energy-intensive than centralisation, because of the potentially large amount of cross-commuting and other travel.

2.3.55 In practice, it is the latter situation that seems to have prevailed in Britain. Decentralisation over the past few decades has already produced suburbs and freestanding settlements with the potential to be self contained, but the level of autonomy typically attained is small, even where self-containment was an explicit objective, as in the new towns. The autonomy of settlements tends to increase with size, but it is also a function of relative isolation. In Kent, for example, three quarters of the county's population live in 18 towns of over 15,000 people. Each town has a mix of facilities, but because they are close together, 'the demand for movement between them is very high'.[116] The most autonomous settlements are the relatively remote new towns, such as Newtown in mid-Wales.[117]

2.3.56 All of this implies that an energy-efficient form of urban development cannot be defined without qualification. The evidence suggests that both centralisation and 'decentralised concentration' are likely to be more energy efficient than peripheral or ex-urban residential development unrelated to jobs and services, but involve different sets of costs.[118]

2.3.57 Planning policies might therefore be aimed at relatively robust forms, involving development in centres large enough to provide access to a good range of jobs and services without the need for long journeys, and with good public transport links to employment and other facilities to offer a viable alternative to the private car. Since, under prevailing conditions of mobility, even quite large mixed developments are unlikely to be self-contained unless they are quite isolated, travel and energy efficiency would best be promoted by integrated development within existing towns and cities, closely related to public transport links.

Energy-efficient transport

2.3.58 The location and form of development also affect choice of transport mode. By reducing the distances which need to be travelled, planning policies could encourage people to walk or cycle, though it would be necessary to integrate land use planning with positive discrimination in favour of these modes, making them feasible not only in terms of distance but also by providing a safe and clean environment.

2.3.59 Land use planning also has a potentially significant role in encouraging modal shift from car to public transport, but this would require greater integration of land use and transport planning. It would be important to consider transport implications at the planning stage of new development, because certain land use patterns are better suited to the efficient and economic operation of public transport than others. Conventional bus and rail, for example, are poorly adapted to serve dispersed, low-density areas typical of residential suburbs[119], whereas relative concentration of homes and facilities maximises accessibility to transport routes and encourages a high load factor.[120] The proximity of work places to public transport facilities may be particularly important: in the Netherlands, car use for the journey to work has proved particularly sensitive to this factor.[121]

2.3.60 Linear urban forms are conducive to public transport, and might entail, for example, broad bands of urban development combining high densities along a bus or light rail route with moderate overall densities (though ribbon development would need to be avoided).[122]

2.3.61 Appropriate planning policies would therefore include discouragement of dispersed, low density residential areas or any significant development heavily dependent on car use; some degree of concentration, though not necessarily *centralisation*, of activities; integration of development with public transport facilities and the maintenance of moderately high densities along transport routes. Where transport networks do not already exist, it would be necessary to plan them in conjunction with the development of land.

2.3.62 A model is provided by the Netherlands *National Environmental Policy Plan* which aims to reduce car use through policies involving the concentration of housing, work, services and leisure facilities.[123] Land use planning will aim to ensure that as much use as possible is made of public transport through a new policy of matching the accessibility profiles of locations with the mobility profiles of businesses or services. Three types of location are distinguished according to their accessibility by public transport. 'Mobility profiles' indicate the characteristics of businesses and services which are of importance for transport, including the number of employees per unit area (from a low of 100 square metres per employee to a high of 40 square metres per employee), dependence on motor vehicles in running of the business (including goods transport) and the number of visitors.

2.3.63 It is acknowledged that 'new or different planning regulations may be necessary' for new locations[124], though new instruments are not considered to be necessary. Provincial administrations will use their powers relating to transport planning and environmental programmes and local authorities can use zoning plans, bye-laws, transport planning, land release, layout of public spaces and measures relating to traffic noise. In the case of existing locations, the possibility of relocating an establishment is not ruled out if it is impossible to match the location with the mobility profile of the business, and it is implied that some planning consents for offices may be cancelled.[125] This location policy is being implemented and existing plans are being tested and brought into line with it as far as possible.[126] It remains to be seen, of course, how successful the policy will be in practice.

2.3.64 As with the reduction of travel needs, appropriate development patterns provide a necessary but not a sufficient condition for the successful operation of public transport. Location policy in isolation is unlikely to have any great impact on modal choice or energy use in transport.

Analytical tools

2.3.65 If land use planning policy is to be proactive as outlined above, there will be a requirement for means of assessing the energy and environmental implications of alternative policies. Some models have already been developed which might be useful in this process. For example, the TEMIS model, designed by the Oko Institute in Germany, can predict the environmental impacts associated with particular patterns of energy use.[127] Useful tools for analysis in land use planning might be developed by combining models like TEMIS with land use/transport models which produce as an output the energy demand associated with different urban development patterns (such as TRANUS, developed at the Open University in the UK in collaboration with the University of Caracas, Venezuela[128]).

Research Needs

2.3.66 Basic research on land use/transport/environment interactions is still required, but is unlikely to be able to answer all the important questions: much depends on variables like the propensity to travel, which are very difficult to predict. Policy studies are needed more urgently, including comparative work. This review suggests that the following theoretical and empirical research would be valuable:

Theoretical work

- Further theoretical work on the energy/environmental implications of different development patterns is required. The possibility of combining models like TRANUS (output – energy requirements of different urban forms) and TEMIS (output – environmental costs associated with different patterns of energy consumption) could usefully be explored, with a view perhaps to producing a package for use by local planning authorities in policy evaluation. The remit of models should extend to the regional scale to include, for example, new settlement options.

- Using land use planning as an instrument of transport policy will have costs and benefits. As with all planning policies, these will be difficult to assess, but it would be useful to establish a framework within which the costs and benefits of policies like that of The Netherlands can be evaluated.

Empirical and theoretical work

- There are opportunities to extend and improve existing research on responses to constraints on travel, much of which was carried out during the 1970s, using new information (for example, on travel patterns and social change) and incorporating public transport investment options. The longer term influence on location of policies such as road pricing needs to be explored.

- Further work on individuals' valuation of mobility would be valuable. This is a critical variable for determining the effectiveness of many policies, particularly land use policies. Social/psychological and/or economic frameworks might be appropriate.

- The interaction of fiscal policies and land use planning policies is an important area for investigation. If traffic and parking are restrained in city centres, for example, what increase in travel costs might be necessary to encourage a change of mode rather than simply a shift of land uses to out of centre locations? Both urban and econometric modelling might be helpful in such an analysis, as would assessment of actual experience. In some countries, development of out-of-town shopping centres has been restrained: if this is combined with travel restraint, how has the overall transport/activity system adjusted?

Empirical work

- A study of the cultural and institutional factors which influence the acceptability of transport policies in different countries would inform comparisons of policy approaches.

- The land use implications of comprehensive traffic management schemes need further analysis both from desk studies of land requirements (for example, for park and ride facilities, other transport interchanges, bus lanes and cycleways) and from actual experience. Similarly, the implications of modal shift need to be translated into land requirements. Although it is clear that at least some new facilities would be required to deal with any significant shift of passengers and freight from road to rail, more explicit links need to be made between percentage shift, increase in rail traffic, the consequent need for new investment and the land take and other land use planning implications. Currently such information is not readily available other than in terms of broad estimates of passenger kilometres and costs, as outlined above. The most useful information from a land use planning perspective would be in a disaggregated form that might predict, for example, the implications for particular regions or counties. Such information might, of course, be sensitive.

- There appears to have been a significant shift in thinking about the objectives and instruments of transport policy in the past few years. A desk study of actual transport policies at local authority level would show what is happening 'on the ground', at least in terms of intent. This might be supplemented by a survey of transport authorities to elucidate the main constraints and perceived constraints on policy implementation. In particular, the concept of integration of land use and transport policy, much advocated, needs to be scrutinised and the main possibilities and constraints, at local and county level, identified.

Summary

2.3.67 The transport sector, and road transport in particular, is likely to be an important focus of efforts to reduce emissions of rfgs, partly because it is the sector in which emissions are growing most rapidly and partly because the 'complementarity factor' is high, given the growing concern about other negative externalities associated with the unrestrained growth of road traffic, including congestion, the contribution to acid pollution and local environmental impacts. Such factors have contributed to pressure for revision of transport policy even before taking account of the sector's contribution to climate change.

2.3.68 But policies involving restraint on traffic growth are certain to be politically contentious, and they impinge on very large numbers of individuals and firms, making agreement and implementation difficult. If the prevailing view is that 'reductions in carbon dioxide emissions from transport could place intolerable restrictions on society'[129], then 'business as usual' is the most likely level of response. Concern about other costs and inefficiencies in the transport system may counter resistance to new policies sufficiently to enable a 'no regrets' strategy to be implemented. An 'enhanced emissions reduction' strategy seems unlikely in the UK unless there is greater certainty about environmental impacts, and concern escalates well beyond current levels.

2.3.69 Policies which might be adopted to reduce rfg emissions from the transport sector are amongst those with the most significant implications for the land use planning system. Links are strong because of the fundamental relationship between land use and transport. Implications arise from land requirements for transport infrastructure, from the impacts of transport policies on development pressures and from the need to integrate land use and transport planning at all scales, involving closer co-operation between the agencies involved, consideration of development pressures which might arise from transport infrastructure and assessment of the transport implications of new development. In all of these areas there is scope for the land use planning system to be both reactive and proactive. Land use planning is also a potential policy instrument which could be employed to encourage the use of energy-efficient forms of transport and to reduce the need for movement in the medium to long term.

2.3.70 The use of land use planning as a policy instrument to modify travel patterns can be envisaged to some extent in all levels of response. Its role is already acknowledged in a number of structure plans, by the Government and by the other major political parties. The Environment White Paper, for example, explicitly acknowledges that 'the way in which towns and cities are planned and laid out, and the physical distances between different types of building and land use'[130] affect the demand for transport, and considers the need for policy guidance 'to guide new development to locations which reduce the need for car journeys and the distances driven, or which permit the choice of more energy efficient public transport – without encouraging more or longer journeys – as an alternative to the private car'.[131] Location policies are unlikely to become effective unless reinforced by other regulatory and fiscal measures.

2.3.71 Many of the time scales are long. Lead times for new transport infrastructure may be up to 10–15 years. More generally, land use planning itself is a long-term strategy and changes to land use patterns can only be brought about in the medium to long term.

2.3.72 Research needs include comparative work on transport policies in different areas of the UK and in other countries, a better understanding of individuals' valuation of mobility and responses to constraints on travel, and assessment of the land use implications of comprehensive traffic management schemes and modal shift. Theoretical work is needed on the energy/environmental implications of alternative development patterns at different scales and on the interaction of fiscal and land use planning policies. There is also need for an assessment, probably qualitative, of the costs and benefits of using land use planning as an instrument of transport policy.

2.4 Combined Heat and Power, Wind and Tidal Power

COMBINED HEAT AND POWER

Combined heat and power, climate change and land use planning

2.4.1 Conventional power stations convert primary fuel into electricity with a maximum efficiency of about 38 per cent. Combined heat and power (CHP), in which some of the heat produced during the process of electricity generation is used for space and water heating, increases the efficiency of conversion of primary fuel to around 80 per cent and therefore leads to reductions in carbon dioxide (and other) emissions per unit of delivered energy. There are basically three types:[132]

(i) urban or large-scale CHP, typically in excess of 100 MWe;

(ii) industrial CHP, typically 4–50 MWe but could be larger; and

(iii) building (or commercial) CHP, typically under 0.5 MWe, to serve one building or a small group of buildings.

2.4.2 In this chapter we consider the potential contribution of CHP to rfg emissions abatement, the current status of the technology and its possible future development in the UK, and the implications of different levels of development for the land use planning system.

Emissions reduction

2.4.3 The environmental benefits of CHP are widely acknowledged but difficult to quantify because CHP operates in all sectors of the economy, on all fuels, and at sizes ranging from around 10 KWe to approximately 1,000 MWe.[133] However, the Department of Energy estimates that gas-fired CHP plant displacing conventional coal-fired generation and heat from predominantly gas fired boilers could save approximately one million tonnes of carbon dioxide for each TWh of electricity generated.[134] Estimates based on technical potential suggest that some 30 GWe CHP capacity might be installed by 2020, out of a total electricity generating capacity (for public supply) of 120 GWe, resulting in a reduction of carbon dioxide emissions of around 15 per cent against a high electricity growth scenario.[135]

2.4.4 Environmental benefits may also be considered in relation to individual schemes. It has been estimated, for example, that a gas-fired CHP project planned for Newcastle-upon-Tyne would reduce carbon dioxide emissions by some 57 per cent compared with coal-fired separate electricity and heat production, and would also result in substantial reductions in emissions of other polluants.[136]

Relevance for land use planning

2.4.5 The most significant land use planning implications arise from urban scale CHP as this involves DH networks. Studies demonstrate that the economic potential for urban-scale CHP/DH depends on the density of development, the degree of mixing of different land uses, the discount rate adopted, assumptions about real fuel prices and the type of area being considered.[137] Connection of existing or new development to such schemes would therefore require careful consideration of urban structural variables which are of key significance in land use planning. Another important factor is the requirement for suitable sites for the CHP stations and a third relates to the role and powers of the planning system in the promotion and development of CHP schemes. These implications are considered in more detail below.

2.4.6 On-site industrial or building/commercial CHP systems are less likely to impinge directly on the planning system because they avoid the need to lay expensive heat distribution networks. However, separate buildings may be required to house CHP plant when it cannot be accommodated internally, for example in a basement, and although these are generally on a small scale, they might not always be welcome and have relevance for development control. Otherwise, implications are indirect. The availability of flexible, package CHP systems may reduce the incentive to pursue urban-scale schemes, and widespread adoption would have implications for energy demand and therefore for land requirements for energy supply facilities. It might also reduce the differential between development costs in different locations. However, there are currently too many uncertainties for these factors to be quantified reliably. Our main emphasis, therefore, is on larger-scale CHP/DH systems, since it is these which have the most direct and significant implications for land use planning.

The current situation in the UK

2.4.7 Only about three per cent of UK electricity supply currently comes from operating CHP plant, a significant part of which is in the industrial sector.[138] While the UK is considered to have the European lead in smaller-scale schemes (less than 0.5 MWe), there has been little progress to date with urban-scale CHP systems. Reasons for slow development of the latter have included the availability of a wide range of indigenous fuels, tariff and taxation structures which have made it difficult for new suppliers to enter the market, and restrictions on local authority capital spending.

2.4.8 In 1979, a working group (the CHP Group) established by the Secretary of State for Energy to explore the feasibility of CHP in the UK concluded that CHP could be the cheapest method of heating British towns and cities in the longer term, and recommended implementation of at least one full-scale scheme. Consequently, during the 1980s, the Energy Efficiency Office (and its predecessors) financed and supported a number of 'lead city' studies, with the object of enabling a free-standing CHP system to be created in at least one major urban area. Support was given in principle to schemes in Edinburgh, Belfast and Leicester. Only that proposed for Leicester achieved viability, but after electricity privatisation it proved impossible to conclude a contract for the electricity sales. Currently, the UK's only city-scale CHP scheme operates in Nottingham.

2.4.9 However, progress has been made with a number of other CHP/DH schemes. In Sheffield, Sheffield Heat and Power, a joint venture involving Sheffield City Council and EKONO Oy of Finland, has laid 17.5 km of a DH network to which some 4,000 homes and the 15 largest consumers of heat in the city centre have already been connected. The primary heat source is the City Council's refuse incinerator. Further development of the DH network is planned and outline planning permission has been granted for construction of a 120 MW combined cycle gas turbine CHP station on the periphery of the urban area, the connection to which will form the arterial structure for further phased expansion of the network.[139]

2.4.10 In Newcastle-Upon-Tyne, Forth Energy Ltd await planning permission for a 150 MW gas-fired CCGT CHP station to supply heat to a number of major users in the city centre. In this case, the CHP station, on the derelict site of a former gasworks, is close to the main heat customers. The City Council supports the project and may become a participant in due course.[140] A further example is the scheme under active consideration in the City of London, which proposes to convert a disused ice store into a power station and to supply both heating and cooling through the network.[141]

2.4.11 The modest progress to date with urban-scale CHP in the UK is in marked contrast to the experience of some other European countries such as Denmark, Finland, Norway and Sweden. Denmark, for example, has pursued a major programme since 1973, building on an already extensive district heating (DH) network. By 1987, 46 per cent of the total demand for heating and domestic hot water was covered by DH, about 27 per cent supplied by CHP, mainly from large central power stations.[142] By the year 2000 a large number of smaller, decentralised CHP stations (fired with a range of fuels including natural gas, biogas, waste and straw) is also expected to be in place and total coverage of DH is likely to increase to 55 per cent of heat supply, including areas of cities and towns with relatively low density of heat demand. Development of DH networks has contributed to substantial reductions in gross energy demand for heating.[143]

2.4.12 Breaking the monopoly of the energy utilities in the UK has significantly altered the institutional and fiscal climate for CHP, with both beneficial and harmful effects. On the positive side there is now less discrepancy between the rates of return required from CHP compared with those from other generation; many on-site industrial CHP schemes are exempt from the fossil fuel levy[144], as are CHP schemes using refuse rather than fossil fuels; electricity suppliers have gained the power to lay heat mains; and the Director General of Electricity supply has been given certain duties and powers in respect of CHP. On the other hand, there is greatly increased uncertainty over income from occasional surpluses of electricity supplied to the Grid and the cost of back-up supplies.[145] On balance, however, the stimulus seems to have been positive, and considerable interest is now being shown in the development of a range of schemes in the UK. Growing environmental awareness, especially concern to reduce emissions of carbon dioxide, is likely to reinforce this trend.

Possible levels of development of CHP

2.4.13 We explore the land use planning implications of CHP/DH with reference to three possible levels of development based on different policy responses.

2.4.14 We regard the 'realistic' potential identified in Energy Paper 58 (Table 12) as a 'business as usual' scenario, in which no special measures to encourage CHP are adopted and development is essentially market led. Even so, there is likely to be modest growth of CHP (especially under higher fuel price assumptions), with quite substantial development in the industrial and buildings/commercial sector, though in both cases growth will be influenced by the cost of back-up electricity and the price offered for any local electricity exports.[146]

2.4.15 Prospects for urban-scale schemes are less encouraging in the absence of specific measures to encourage their development. Progress may be inhibited by the eight year time limit on the non fossil fuel obligation (NFFO), which provides a base for many refuse-based and other renewable energy

Table 12 'Realistic' potential for CHP

	Potential TWh		CO₂ Savings mt	
	2005	2020	2005	2020
Industry and Public/Commercial* (on-site CHP)	25–34	42–55	25–34	42–55
DH/domestic** (off-site CHP)	2.5	7.3	2	7

Source: Department of Energy 1989 (Energy Paper 58)
* Realistic potential estimated on base scenarios (central growth) with low and high fuel price variants and some detailed consideration of market potential within the sectors.
** Assumes no economic prospects for micro-CHP in the domestic sector – all contribution is from DH. Base scenarios assume coal fired CHP plant for DH, so no significant carbon dioxide savings result (benefits from increased efficiency has to be offset by switch to coal from other fuel for heating). Savings shown here assume CCGT or other heat source, such as refuse incineration.

CHP schemes. Other problems include the price regime for electricity, which currently makes it difficult to use this income to finance the heat distribution network, and the inability of the market to place a figure on the wider environmental benefits of heat distribution systems. The figures suggest perhaps 0.6 GWe CHP/DH capacity by 2005 and 1.7 GWe capacity by 2020. For illustration, this might translate into three or four schemes of the Newcastle/Sheffield scale by 2005 and perhaps a dozen such schemes by 2020.

2.4.16 Some pressure is already apparent, however, for policies to encourage the development of CHP at a faster rate than that which might occur under purely market-led conditions. A 'no regrets' strategy might involve at least minimising barriers which prevent the economic energy-saving potential of the technology from being realised (involving, for example, a key role for the Office of Electricity Regulation [OFFER]) and, even before carbon dioxide abatement is taken into account, other benefits of CHP might justify a certain amount of further active encouragement. For example, CHP leads to significant reductions in acid emissions, could provide a cost-effective way of dealing with municipal waste and has also been seen as a factor in inner city regeneration and the provision of employment opportunities (the Newcastle scheme would generate 750–900 person-years of employment during construction, followed by 40–80 permanent positions and has been promoted partly as a 'showcase' for local skills[147]). It has also been advocated as a cost-effective way of combating problems of fuel poverty in local authority housing.[148]

2.4.17 We might envisage, therefore, that in a 'no regrets' scenario, measures might be taken to minimise market imperfections, ways would be found to reduce the effects of uncertain electricity prices and the NFFO and fossil fuel levy might be used to encourage all CHP schemes. Such steps have already been proposed by the Energy Committee, which has argued that the modest increases in CHP capacity envisaged by the Secretary of State for Energy in his evidence to the Committee 'would not . . . adequately reflect the environmental advantages of CHP'.[149]

2.4.18 The CHP Association suggests that if matters such as the uncertain impact of the NFFO and the economics of heat distribution were resolved 'then the environmental case for CHP would undoubtedly lead to the wider development of CHP in urban areas'.[150]

2.4.19 In an 'enhanced emissions reduction' scenario, CHP would be seen as an instrument of carbon dioxide abatement policy and all of the above measures proposed by the Energy Committee would be adopted. These measures are justified, in the view of the Committee, '[n]ow that the government is willing to set a target for carbon dioxide emissions which it believes will impose costs on the economy'.[151] Additional ways of encouraging the development of urban-scale CHP (including institutional and legal changes and the involvement of the land use planning system, as in Denmark) might be pursued in this scenario, and the introduction of a carbon or energy tax, at the national and/or European scale would provide a further stimulus. Something close to the estimate based on technical potential might be achieved.

2.4.20 It is assumed in Energy Paper 58 that no more than 50 per cent of electricity generation capacity could support CHP and that about half this technical potential might be achievable in practice (full technical potential cannot be achieved for a number of reasons). This leads to the possibility of installed CHP capacity of 22 GWe in 2005 and 30 GWe in 2020. However, it is envisaged that only 10 GWe would be connected to district heating schemes, the rest being split between industry (15 GWe) and buildings (5 GWe). Carbon dioxide savings of around 110 mt in 2005 and 150 mt in 2020 would result, representing, by 2020, some 15 per cent of all UK carbon dioxide emissions against high growth in electricity demand. This might imply (for illustration) some 60 or 70 schemes on the Newcastle/Sheffield scale by 2020.

Land use planning implications

2.4.21 The sensitivity of the land use planning system to the further development of CHP/DH can be addressed in relation to three important sets of issues:

(i) the implications of CHP for urban form (or, conversely, the effect of urban form on the viability of CHP);

(ii) the requirement for sites, primarily for power stations, but also for smaller-scale CHP facilities; and

(iii) the institutional role of land use planning and in particular the relationship with energy utilities and heat supply planning.

CHP and urban form

2.4.22 During the 1970s the CHP Group conducted theoretical analyses of the factors affecting the economic viability of CHP, including certain urban structural factors such as density and land use mix.[152] More detailed analyses of real cities was subsequently conducted in the 'lead city' studies.[153]

2.4.23 The CHP Group estimated costs for three hypothetical situations – a small 'green field' development (10,000 people), an existing small city (100,000 people) and an existing large city (one million people) – and compared them with the costs of individual gas-fired central heating for the new development and with the existing fuel mix in the other cases.

2.4.24 Results suggested that the economics of urban-scale CHP are sensitive to density, but this sensitivity is mediated by other factors. For example, in the case of the existing small city, with a 10 per cent discount rate (over a 60 year period) and assuming constant real fuel prices, the break even density was more than 250 dwellings per hectare. Reducing the discount rate to 5 per cent, or assuming that real fuel prices will double every 18 years, reduced the break even density to about 50 dwellings per hectare in each case (Figure 15). These results were obtained assuming a modified existing power station 15 km from the edge of the scheme (costs are sensitive to this assumption).

2.4.25 In the green field case, the break even density was about 75 dwellings per hectare with a 10 per cent discount rate and constant real fuel prices, coming down to less than 25 dwellings per hectare or 37 dwellings per hectare by modifying the discount rate or fuel price assumptions as above.[154] The economics are more favourable for green field (i.e. new) development because heat mains and connections can be installed at the point of construction.

2.4.26 The inverse relationship between development density and network costs was confirmed in the subsequent studies of real cities.[155] This work concentrated on 'high density heat load' areas, defined as those having a net density of at least 20 MW/km[2], which would be typical of areas with dwelling densities of 44 or more dwellings per hectare. However, circumstances have changed in the intervening period (for example, fossil fuel costs have fallen, but there is more concern to internalise environmental costs). It is therefore difficult to draw conclusions about threshold densities, and there seem to be no current operational figures.[156] The cost of service mains is also important and varies not only with density but with factors such as built form, because of the ease of routing mains.

2.4.27 The other significant structural factor is a mix of different land uses – residential, industrial and commercial – which spreads the demand for heat and electricity and improves the viability of CHP schemes. A large and stable heat load is now the key requirement, since electricity can be sold to the grid (though negotation of contracts has, as noted above, presented an obstacle in at least one case).

Figure 15   Costs of CHP, small city development with 10 per cent discount rate

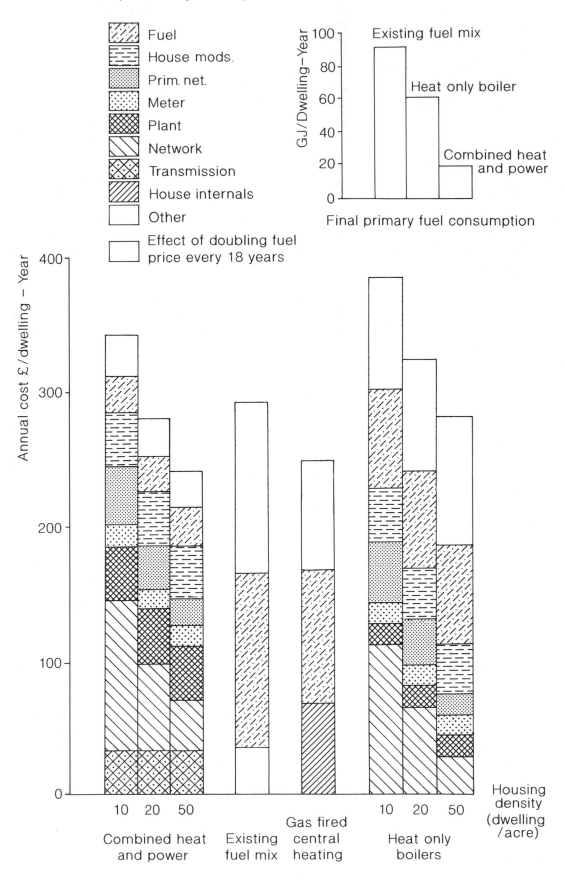

Source: Combined Heat and Power Group, 1977

2.4.28 These findings imply that for urban-scale CHP schemes, development should ideally be dense, mixed, on a reasonably large-scale and capable of being reached by heat mains without significant disruption. Though in theory CHP is more viable, because heat mains can be installed more cheaply, on green field sites, lack of powers to compel firms or households to connect to the network (discussed below) would seem to present an obstacle in areas where there is no established development.[157] In existing urban areas, it might be possible to negotiate a large and stable core heat load in advance, and many of the urban structural requirements could normally be met. Additional development within the urban area might then further improve the economics of the scheme. Because of the costs involved in routing the heat mains, much would depend in any case on the location of the power station in relation to the areas being served.

2.4.29 Where new development is planned which might be connected to an existing or future DH network, consideration needs to be given to factors such as density, built form and the mixing of land uses. In relation to both new and existing development, land use planners might become involved in defining critical minimum thresholds for CHP systems. There is very little experience of such planning in the UK to date, partly because there are so few existing CHP/DH schemes (where the parameters would be known) and partly because land use planning and the planning of energy supply are conducted as largely separate exercises. This last point raises a wider issue which is discussed in more detail below.

Site requirements

2.4.30 Further development of CHP/DH will lead to a requirement for sites for CHP stations. In the case of schemes serving existing built up areas, this will be the main implication for the land use planning system. Land requirements for typical schemes will be relatively small. The CHP station in Newcastle-Upon-Tyne, for example, will require one or two hectares of land to accommodate the main and ancillary buildings. Incoming gas supply and outgoing heat and electricity circuits will be laid underground. Lead times are expected to be short: the current project was initiated in 1988 (though other possibilities had been explored in Newcastle throughout the 1980s), and the scheme is expected to be operational by the mid-1990s. However, this timescale may be extended by potential problems over NO_x emissions, which are a cause for concern because of the topographical relationship of the site to nearby high rise flats. Power station construction is expected to take about two years.[158] The CHP station planned for the Sheffield scheme is on a site outside the main urban area.

2.4.31 Siting of any new facilities, even very small ones, can be contentious: this depends very much upon the specific site and circumstances. Refuse-based schemes, which currently benefit from the NFFO, probably need to be big enough to support two or even three furnaces (so that one can be out of action if necessary) and are likely to be the most difficult in terms of siting.

2.4.32 The land use planning system could be purely reactive in relation to site requirements, or it might be proactive in terms of identifying potential sites for new facilities (in Newcastle, both the Urban Development Corporation and the City Planning Department have played an active role). In an 'enhanced emissions reduction' scenario, it is highly likely that the planning system would need to adopt a positive role in identifying sites suitable for CHP facilities in development plans. Of considerable interest here is the existence of potentially suitable sites – such as disused power station or gas holder sites – in or close to urban areas where the heat load is likely to make CHP/DH viable.

2.4.33 As noted above, CHP on the scale of buildings might also involve site requirements and although these are modest, applications may become quite numerous and clearly involve development control issues at the local scale.

Institutional issues

2.4.34 The implications of urban-scale CHP/DH for the built environment suggest that if this technology is introduced on a significant scale greater integration of land use planning and the planning of energy supply might lead to better overall system efficiencies. In Denmark, municipal authorities co-operate with utilities (for example, natural gas companies and district heating plants) to produce heat supply plans, and the process provides for comprehensive public hearing and information phases. County councils must ensure that municipal heat plans are consistent with regional heat plans, which are approved by the Minister of Energy. Under the 1979 Heat Supply Act, town councils have the right to stipulate that all potential consumers of DH must be connected: in Kalundborg, for example, this right was exercised in 1984, requiring connection by 1993.[159] In the case of heat supply, the benefits of efficient systems are considered to outweigh those of consumer choice.

2.4.35 There is no formal mechanism in the UK for such integration. The existence post-privatisation of a multiplicity of energy suppliers may make voluntary co-operation – and indeed participation in projects – by local authorities more likely; on the other hand, it increases the number of actors involved and makes negotiations more complex. Any extensive development of CHP/DH may stimulate consideration of the institutional framework and the role and powers of the land use planning system in the planning of heat supply, but arguably unless the latter are changed, extensive development of urban-scale schemes is in any case unlikely.

Research needs

2.4.36 Experience with existing CHP schemes in the UK needs to be carefully monitored, especially the role they might play in attracting development to inner city areas because of low energy costs. Comparison with the situation in other countries would also be informative, for example a comparative analysis of the role of the land use planning system in CHP/DH development in Denmark and the UK would help to clarify the significance of different cultural and political factors, and institutional relationships.

2.4.37 A desk study of suitable sites for power stations in or on the fringes of a sample of towns and cities would be useful, as would consideration of the use of such sites for CHP/DH stations in relation to other potential uses.

2.4.38 More generally, the benefits and costs of proactive involvement of land use planning in the promotion of CHP/DH need to be explored. If CHP develops on any extensive scale, there is likely to be a need for policy guidance which would be informed by the results of such research.

Summary

2.4.39 Limited development of urban-scale CHP/DH – perhaps a handful of schemes – is likely in a 'business as usual' scenario. 'No regrets' and 'enhanced emissions reduction' strategies would stimulate more extensive development, the latter case involving perhaps 60 or 70 CHP/DH schemes in towns and cities. Some tens of schemes might be envisaged in the 'no regrets' situation. Currently the prospects for urban-scale CHP are limited by the fiscal environment, and to some extent by considerations of consumer choice. On the other hand, there is complementarity with a number of social and environmental objectives and significant technical potential to reduce carbon dioxide emissions (15 per cent by 2020). The 'no regrets' strategy may not be unrealistic in the medium term, but the level of development implied by the 'enhanced emissions reduction' scenario seems unlikely. Even in the 'business as usual' strategy, however, there is likely to be considerable development of smaller-scale CHP schemes.

2.4.40 There are strong links with land use planning because of the significance of urban structural variables, siting requirements and institutional implications. Ideally, urban areas to be served by CHP/DH should be relatively dense, mixed, on a reasonably large scale and capable of being reached by heat mains without significant disruption elsewhere in the urban system. However, much depends on the fiscal environment (fuel prices, investment criteria, financing etc.) and on the specific characteristics of a scheme (for example proximity of power station).

2.4.41 There are siting requirements for power stations, and also for smaller-scale CHP facilities. A 150 MWe CCGT CHP station requires one or two hectares of land. Environmental impacts are not great, but the need for urban sites may arouse controversy and even small-scale facilities will raise issues for development control.

2.4.42 The involvement of the land use planning system is likely to increase in close relation with the extent of CHP/DH development, from minimal (depending on individual planning authorities) in a 'business as usual' scenario to extensive and possibly proactive in an 'enhanced emissions reduction' scenario. Immediate implications are not substantial, but these may build in the medium term, 10–15 years.

2.4.43 A number of significant time thresholds can be identified. The NFFO is a stimulus to refuse-based schemes and will be in place until 1998: it may be extended in scope and time scale. A realistic time threshold for development of an urban-scale CHP/DH scheme from conception to operation is probably 10–15 years, though there is little experience to date on which to base this estimate. Controversy over siting the power station might extend this timetable. The timing of major urban infrastructural programmes (for example road building or renewal of sewerage systems) is important as the simultaneous laying of heat mains would reduce overall costs. This will vary from place to place. In Newcastle-Upon-Tyne, a plan to lay heat mains in conjunction with the construction of a major new road had to be abandoned because of programming difficulties; instead, the mains will be laid along roads parallel to the route.

2.4.44 A minimum role for land use planning would be to react to proposals for power station (and smaller-scale) developments as they occur. In a more proactive role, local planning authorities might seek to identify suitable sites for CHP stations. They might also seek to encourage CHP/DH development as part of overall urban renewal strategy (the role of urban development corporations is important here) and to encourage new development that would benefit from CHP scheme and be compatible with it in terms of heat load. In this sense land use planning could itself become a policy instrument in the promotion of CHP/DH schemes. These activities would not require new powers, though as more local planning authorities were confronted with the possibility of CHP/DH development, some policy guidance might become necessary.

2.4.45 Extensive development of CHP/DH might stimulate, or even require, institutional change to effect the closer integration of land use planning and energy supply planning in relevant towns and cities. Additional powers, for example the ability to specify heating systems in new buildings, might need to be explored.

2.4.46 Proactive planning policies would involve some costs, for example in identifying (reserving) sites for power stations as opposed to other purposes or in compelling potential customers to connect to DH network if this became possible. The opportunity costs involved, as well as the administrative costs, would need to be weighed against the benefits, including the environmental benefits, of a viable, operational CHP/DH scheme.

2.4.47 Research needs focus on monitoring experience in the UK, international comparative work, and further elucidation of siting requirements and availability. There is also a need for assessment of the costs and benefits of adopting a more proactive stance towards CHP within the planning system, including the possibility of additional powers such as the ability to specify heating systems.

RENEWABLE ENERGY: WIND AND TIDAL POWER

2.4.48 Though the likelihood of extensive development of wind and tidal power in the short to medium term in the UK is not great, we consider these energy sources here because of their relatively strong links with the land use planning system. In each case we outline the current state of development and the major land use planning implications.

Wind energy in the UK

2.4.49 Onshore wind power is 'currently emerging as one of the more promising renewable energy sources for electricity generation in the UK'[160] and demonstration wind farms are already planned at several sites, ranging from Cornwall to Cumbria. The Secretary of State for Energy has indicated that in autumn 1991, a specific Order under the NFFO will be made for the subsequent year for the regional electricity companies (RECs) to take 25–50 MWe of wind-generated power (compared with a 12 MWe contribution from this source currently).[161]

2.4.50 Wind energy contributes to the diversification of electricity supply sources, and is seen as one way of reducing fossil fuel consumption and the consequent emission of rfgs. The overall contribution to carbon dioxide emissions abatement is likely to be relatively small. It is calculated, for example, that a wind farm producing 25 million kWh of electricity per year could abate carbon dioxide emissions by some 25,000 tonnes.[162] Though Energy Paper 58 suggests a maximum build rate capacity of 600 MWe of onshore wind generation from 1995, (with installed capacity reaching 6 GW by 2005 and 15 GW by 2020), actual achievement of such a rate would be likely only under a fairly extreme 'enhanced emissions reduction' scenario where economic circumstances or NFFO orders gave special opportunities to wind power. Realistically, installed capacity is likely to be considerably less than this, but nevertheless raises some important issues for the land use planning system.

Land use planning implications of on-shore wind energy

2.4.51 The UK planning system is currently experiencing the first processing of applications for consent to construct commercial wind farms, which raise significant issues related to land take and visual intrusion.

2.4.52 It is often implied that wind-generated electricity requires large amounts of land. For example, National Power suggests a requirement of 37,500 ha of land per GWe[163] (Figure 16). However, such figures may be misleading, because the total *developed* area of a wind farm will be very much smaller than the overall site area occupied by the generators, perhaps of the order of 1 per cent, and agricultural use is possible on the land between the wind generators.[164] Many other forms of development would clearly be precluded, but are in any case relatively unlikely in the areas suitable for wind generation.

Figure 16 Comparative scale to illustrate land use implications of on-shore windpower to a significant energy contribution

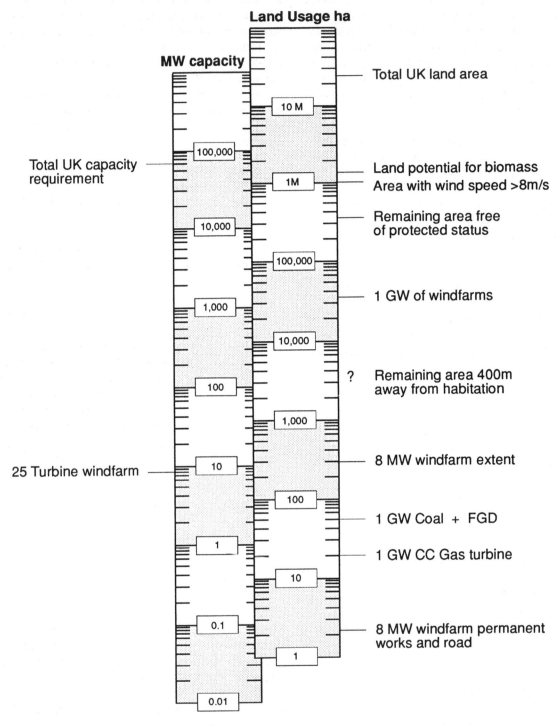

Source : Manning 1990

Note : Extent of windfarms is total land area.
Land area used by turbines is much
smaller and other uses (eg agriculture)
remain possible in between

2.4.53 While land take *per se* may not be of major concern, the specific siting requirements associated with wind generation are an important planning issue and are already proving controversial because of visual impact. Wind turbine generators require high and consistent average wind speeds and need to be placed in treeless, open exposed locations in the countryside 'where most other forms of development have usually been resisted'.[165] In particular, the planning system has tended to presume against developments on hill top sites.

2.4.54 The currently-quoted lowest mean annual wind speed for economic wind generation is 7.5 m/sec. About 80% of the land area in the UK within this limit is in designated areas such as national parks, and further areas would be visible from them. It has been argued that the current pricing mechanism of the NFFO militates against development on sites with lower windspeeds.[166] Changes in the basis of cost appraisal could significantly relax the areal constraint imposed by current windspeed requirements. Such a relaxation could have the effect of bringing forward more schemes, but might also make it easier to avoid areas where visual intrusion is considered to be particularly serious.

2.4.55 Though the maximum technical build scenario presented in Energy Paper 58 is unlikely except in a rather extreme 'enhanced emissions reduction' scenario, the controversial nature of many potential schemes, and the lack of experience of the planning system with developments of this kind, makes wind energy an important and fairly urgent matter for the land use planning system. This is particularly the case since the 1998 deadline on the NFFO may bring forward a number of schemes in the short term. The need for guidance has already been recognised, and planning policy guidance on renewable energy generally was issued at the end of 1991, after completion of this report.

Potential for tidal power in the UK

2.4.56 Tidal power exploits the rotational inertia of the earth and can be regarded as a renewable resource. Geomorphological factors make the west coast of Britain an especially favourable location for tidal generation. Energy Paper 58 presented a possibility of up to 18.3 TWh of generation by 2005 (the Severn and Mersey schemes) and 23.7 TWh by 2020, corresponding to an 'enhanced emissions reduction scenario'. Overall, about 90% of the country's technical tidal potential is at eight large sites, with a further 34 sites providing the remaining 10%.

2.4.57 The capital-intensive nature of tidal barrages is a constraint on their development in the absence of public sector funding, and Energy Paper 58 also acknowledges uncertainties about their environmental acceptability. A crash programme of barrage construction on the scale presented in the technical limits scenario of Energy Paper 58 must be viewed as unlikely, even under an 'enhanced emissions reduction' scenario, because of the alternative availability of other rfg emission reduction options. Any proposals which do come forward, however, will raise substantial issues for the land use planning system.

Land use planning implications of tidal power

2.4.58 Tidal barrage construction will have major local and regional implications and will raise many issues relating to environmental impacts, infrastructure requirements and regional economic effects. Many of the issues raised would be typical of major infrastructural development projects and therefore not unfamiliar to the planning system. Clearly there is a need for awareness of the implications, and for co-operation between neighbouring authorities, especially in those areas with the most favoured sites. Planning considerations are themselves likely to represent a constraint on the development of this energy option. This is an area where the planning system needs to keep a close watching brief on likely developments and their land use planning implications. Developments on a major scale, such as the Severn barrage, will require regional level consideration.

Research needs: wind and tidal energy

2.4.59 Wind energy is a new technology raising some novel and controversial as well as some familiar issues for land use planning. Methodologies, such as Environmental Assessment and landscape evaluation techniques already exist, though they remain controversial. Proposals for wind farms might therefore provide excellent test cases for further development, improvement and testing of the relevant techniques.

2.4.60 The sensitivity of wind energy viability to alternative pricing mechanisms under the NFFO and the mapping of the implications would be a worthwhile exercise. Consideration may also need to be given to overall planning guidelines, identifying areas of suitability for wind energy development as well as areas where such development would not normally be permitted.

2.4.61   We have not identified specific new research needs in relation to tidal power, but note that specific needs are likely to materialise as the prospects for this energy source become clearer.

2.5 Passive Solar and Microclimatic Design of Buildings

Buildings, climate change and land use planning

2.5.1 Energy consumption in buildings (for heating, lighting and electrical appliances) accounts for nearly half of Britain's total energy use.[167] Space heating accounts for the most significant proportion of this demand, and contributes around a quarter of total UK carbon dioxide emissions.[168] Reducing energy consumption in buildings, particularly for space heating, could therefore make a major contribution to rfg emissions abatement.

2.5.2 Energy consumption in buildings has been the subject of a considerable amount of attention, though many measures to improve energy efficiency do not obviously impinge on the planning system. In this chapter, we focus on measures which affect building design and the form of development.

Relevance for land use planning

2.5.3 The most significant of these measures relate to built form and passive solar and microclimatic design (Table 13). Design, layout and orientation, for example, determine the extent to which solar radiation and microclimate can be used to reduce conventional energy requirements. Policies to encourage or require consideration of such factors in development would influence the fine grain of urban structure and would therefore have significant implications for land use planning. These arise both from the need to take new factors into account in development control and from the potential use of land use planning as a policy instrument to encourage energy-conscious development.

2.5.4 Other measures to improve efficiency in buildings might also have land use planning implications. In particular, high standards of insulation could affect the design and appearance of both new and existing buildings. Large-scale housing renovation programmes might, for example, include measures such as external wall insulation and could raise questions about the role of local planning authorities in matters which are traditionally dealt with through the building regulations. Certainly planners need to be aware of such developments, but currently insulation measures do not have major land use planning implications.

2.5.5 We also focus in this chapter on the domestic sector where the factors listed in Table 13 are likely to have most impact and where most of the relevant research has been carried out. However, the concepts are often applicable to other buildings such as offices

Table 13 Structural variables affecting space heating requirements at the micro-scale

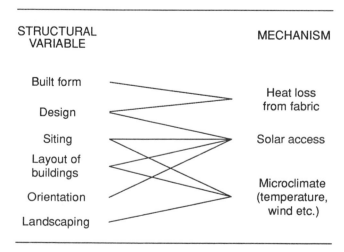

STRUCTURAL VARIABLE	MECHANISM
Built form	
Design	Heat loss from fabric
Siting	Solar access
Layout of buildings	
Orientation	Microclimate (temperature, wind etc.)
Landscaping	

59

and schools. Our emphasis is on new buildings rather than the existing building stock, since the relevant characteristics must normally be incorporated at the time of construction. Some features, such as window design, conservatories, and landscaping are exceptions to this and, as noted above, measures such as insulation can be incorporated into renovation programmes and may to some extent impinge on the land use planning system.

Potential emissions abatement

2.5.6 Policies to improve efficiency in domestic space heating generally might influence some 12–13 per cent of UK carbon dioxide emissions.[169] If non-domestic buildings are included, estimates suggest that around 25 per cent of carbon dioxide emissions might be affected. However, since we are concerned with a sub-set of measures mainly incorporated in new build, and average turnover in the housing stock is at the rate of about one per cent per annum[170], the impact of relevant policies on carbon dioxide emissions will be modest and realised in the medium to long term. Nevertheless, since many of the measures are likely to be cost-effective, it is important to explore their implications for the land use planning system.

2.5.7 We consider first the impact of built form and passive solar and microclimatic design on energy consumption. The main implications for urban form also emerge in this assessment, since structural factors are an integral part of the energy efficiency measures. We then outline three scenarios involving different levels of adoption of the principles of energy-conscious design, before considering the land use planning implications of such measures.

Energy-conscious design: effects on energy consumption and urban form

2.5.8 The influence of built form and passive solar design on energy consumption are relatively well-documented; empirical evidence is available as well as results of extensive experimentation with computer models. In other cases, such as tree planting and landscaping to control microclimate, the results of reliable empirical testing are still awaited.

Built form

2.5.9 Built form exerts a systematic influence on energy requirements for space heating. Other things being equal, detached houses require as much as three times the energy input of intermediate flats.[171] Though in practice a large number of variables determine heating requirements[172], a trend towards built forms like terraced housing or low rise flats could result in significant reductions in energy demand.

Such a trend would imply generally higher net densities.

2.5.10 Many factors other than energy efficiency determine built form and are likely to continue to do so, but it is worth noting that smaller housing units, which are very often in the form of terraces or flats, are particularly suited to meeting projected household pressures. By the year 2001, 85 per cent of new households will be accounted for by single people.[173] The opportunity to take advantage of energy-efficient built forms may therefore be considerable even in a 'business as usual' scenario.

Passive solar design

2.5.11 The harnessing of solar energy by appropriate design (passive solar energy) can lead to significant savings in conventional fuel at little or no economic or environmental cost. There are two separate but related elements to consider. First, houses can be designed to take advantage of solar gain, for example by including wide frontages, large glazing areas on the south elevation and conservatories. Such buildings are often referred to as 'passive solar houses'. The other element relates to the siting, orientation and layout of buildings to maximise solar gain and avoid overshadowing. Even conventional houses can take advantage of these factors to make small energy savings (of the order of one per cent), but they become more critical for houses designed with passive solar energy in mind. For none of the potential savings from solar design to be lost, solar houses must face ±30 degrees of south and obstruction on the south side of buildings should be avoided.[174]

2.5.12 Empirical evidence demonstrates that in the optimal situation (passive solar houses on an ideal site) energy demand for space heating might be reduced by 11–12 per cent. Research suggests that with attention to layout and orientation, 80 per cent of these maximum possible savings can be achieved in passive solar houses on real sites with densities up to 40 dwellings per hectare.[175] At higher densities it becomes difficult to avoid some houses being seriously obstructed or having poor orientation. The most significant constraints are likley to occur on urban sites which tend to be small (typicaly 0.5 hectares), developed to a high density (40–80dph) and overshaded by existing buildings.

2.5.13 To take full advantage of passive solar energy entails some departure from conventional practice in design and layout and there are implications for development densities (Table 14), but the advantages of passive solar gain could potentially be realised in a significant proportion of modern housing development. At typical building densities

Table 14 Comparison between solar and conventional layout

> Road structure will be influenced by the need to orientate houses towards (i.e. within 30 degrees of) the South; ideally estate roads will run East/West with linking roads running North/South.
>
> Positioning of houses within plots will vary to avoid overshadowing: in general, houses will be situated towards the North end of plots.
>
> Plot shapes will be influenced by orientation requirements and the wider house frontages resulting from passive solar design.
>
> More attention has to be paid to tree planting, for example evergreens to the North of the house and deciduous varieties to the South.
>
> Where there is a mix of dwelling types care has to be taken to avoid overshadowing: for example, it may be necessary to site bungalows to the South of two-storey houses and taller buildings at northern boundaries.
>
> To overcome the uniform effect of all houses appearing to face the same way more attention needs to be paid to the juxtaposition of house types and to the spaces between dwellings.
>
> When pedestrian and vehicle access is from the South, privacy of principal rooms may be effected by side entry to the houses. Typically this will mean more gable ends facing onto roads.

Source: NBA Tectonics, 1988

(around 25 dwellings per hectare for private sector development in the UK) criteria for passive solar design do not present major difficulties and do not conflict with general planning considerations such as those relating to daylight and privacy, though there may be conflicts on specific sites (for example, tree preservation orders may mean that layout cannot be optimised). The most important requirement is that constraints are taken into account early enough in the planning process to influence key factors like road orientation.

2.5.14 For individual buildings and groups of buildings benefits of passive solar design in terms of energy and money saving could be substantial. NBA Tectonics estimated that the *national* primary energy saving after 20 years following the gradual introduction of passive solar house design and layout principles would be of the order of 0.2mtce per annum, with the cumulative energy saving over the 20 years being about 1.5mtce. This is small in relation to current primary energy consumption (c. 328mtce) though not insignificant in absolute terms. The contribution to carbon dioxide emissions abatement from these measures must also therefore be small, but it may be obtainable at no (direct) cost: passive solar estates need not cost any more to construct than conventional schemes.

Other microclimatic considerations

2.5.15 Attention to microclimate can reduce heat loss from buildings in a number of ways, for example by controlling wind speed and by raising external ambient temperatures. Appropriate measures include careful siting, the use of particular materials, attention to building layout, landscaping and the planting of shelter belts of trees (Table 15). The influence of these factors on energy demand is less well researched than passive solar design, but preliminary results suggest that savings might be of the order of at least five per cent and perhaps considerably more on exposed sites[176]. Ideally, microclimatic considerations would also influence the *location* of new development, favouring sites with good microclimatic potential for housing, shopping and open air leisure facilities, for example.[177] However, in most urban areas where land is scarce, the important requirement will be to make the best use of microclimate on sites selected for other reasons. Detailed guidelines are now available in the UK.[178]

2.5.16 As with passive solar design, wind control and other features designed to optimise microclimate could largely be achieved by 'fine tuning' present planning practice.[179] There might, however, be conflict with some visual aspects of design, for example the desire for variety in form, scale and space, and for views. Wind control and solar access may sometimes be in conflict with each other, and both raise issues of rights and constraints, since one person's building or wind shelter can be another's solar obstruction. All such considerations have implications for planning

Table 15 Means of enhancing microclimate in the spaces around buildings

> **Wind Protection**
>
> Protect from dominant or cold winds
>
> Prevent buildings and landscape features from generating unacceptable wind turbulence
>
> Protect from driving rain and snow
>
> Protect from cold air 'drainage' (katabatic flows) at night
>
> (But retain enough air movement to disperse pollutants)
>
> **Features**
>
> Provide external thermal mass to moderate temperature extremes
>
> Use vegetation for sun-shading and wind protection; transpiration helps moderate high temperatures in summer
>
> Provide surfaces that drain and dry readily
>
> Provide water for summer cooling by evaporation (pools, fountains etc.)

Source: BRE, 1990

education, planning policies and development control.

Prospects for implementation of energy-conscious design

2.5.17 Currently the effect of microstructural factors on energy demand receives no statutory consideration in the development process. These factors are not covered by the building regulations and it is unlikely that they would stand as material considerations in development control. A recent survey of local planning authorities showed that while many were aware of the advantages of energy-conscious design and site planning, and some have included appropriate policies in structure and/or local plans, they felt that refusal of, or attachment of conditions to, planning consent on these grounds would be unlikely to be upheld on appeal and might result in costs being awarded against the planning authority[180].

2.5.18 The 1990 Environment White Paper considers briefly the potential for passive solar design, and acknowledges that 'simple measures . . . can lead to major reductions in the energy needed for heating, cooling and lighting offices, schools and hospitals'. It points to continuing research and accepts the need 'to increase awareness of the benefits among developers, designers and clients'.[181] No specific policies are proposed, however, and we therefore assume that in a 'business as usual' scenario, application of passive solar and microclimatic design principles would continue to be on a voluntary basis by developers and on a small scale. Pressures from within the architectural and planning professions and from energy and environmental groups might lead to some diffusion of ideas and a gradual increase in energy-conscious design practice over time. Progress with the energy-labelling of buildings would help to promote this awareness.

2.5.19 In a scenario in which policies are pursued on a 'no regrets' basis, certain measures would be pursued vigorously, since they deliver benefits (albeit rather slowly) but need involve no additional construction costs. NBA Tectonics estimated that at the densities at which they are normally built, 100 per cent of detached and semi-detached houses and bungalows, 50 per cent of terraced houses and 25 per cent of flats could achieve the full energy saving potential from passive solar design.[182] They then assumed increasing take up over the next twenty years, rising to 75 per cent in the public sector and 50 per cent in the private sector, and applied correction factors to reflect the reduction in solar benefit from site and climatic factors in different regions (South, 90 per cent; North 75 per cent; Scotland 50 per cent).

These are the assumptions which led to the cumulative savings of 1.5mtce after twenty years and an annual saving thereafter of 0.2mtce, and they might reasonably constitute a 'no regrets' scenario.

2.5.20 To achieve this level of take up, we would envisage at least extensive information/exhortation to incorporate principles of energy-conscious design in new development, including planning policy guidance, and possibly a statutory requirement to take account of these factors in planning applications and development control. In response to a recommendation from the House of Commons Energy Committee that 'applicants for planning permission for new buildings be required to state what account they have taken of the energy efficiency aspects of layout and design'[183] the Government has already undertaken to consider guidance for local planning authorities on these matters.[184] Progress with the energy labelling of buildings could provide an additional stimulus to energy-conscious design at the construction stage. However, in the case of any conflict with other objectives (for example, amenity), energy efficiency is likely to receive relatively low priority in a 'no regrets' scenario.

2.5.21 In an 'enhanced emissions reduction' scenario, energy efficiency in buildings would be pursued more vigorously as an instrument of environmental policy, according to the philosophy that the sum of the relatively small environmental benefits accruing from many individual measures over time would be significant. Take up would be greater in this scenario because it would be a requirement that such factors were taken into account and greater emphasis might be given to them in the development control process. Even so, strict implementation is unlikely where there is conflict with other objectives because the 'cost' would then be perceived to be high in relation to the modest and long term reductions in carbon dioxide emissions to be achieved by microstructural measures. Take up would therefore be greater than in the 'no regrets' case, especially in the private sector, but is unlikely to reach 100 per cent of potential.

Land use planning implications

2.5.22 Measures to improve energy efficiency through energy-conscious design and layout of buildings have direct links with land use planning in three ways:

- voluntary application of energy-conscious design principles will raise issues for development control;

- forward planning and development control are likely to be policy instruments if national policy requires that energy-conscious design principles are taken into account; and

- wider implications arise from the need to integrate land use planning with the planning of energy supply/efficiency.

Voluntary application

2.5.23   In a 'business as usual' scenario, there is likely to be some diffusion of energy-conscious design practice and the land use planning system would need to respond to this. Existing planning regulations are not thought to exert a major constraining influence on passive solar or microclimatic design, but some adjustments are needed to conventional thinking and practice, for example on road layout, building lines, height restrictions, appearance and tree preservation and planting (see Tables 14 and 15). Local planning authorities may wish to include such considerations in design guides. An interesting precedent has occurred in relation to solar panels and potential conflicts with Conservation Area objectives: Brighton District Council, for example, has produced design guidelines to cover this issue.

2.5.24   Current trends suggest that, even in this scenario, local planning authorities will seek increasingly to adopt energy-related policies in this context, though the effectiveness of such policies may not be great in the face of resistance from volume housebuilders and lack of any statutory guidance or support. Dissemination of information and best practice within the profession would be of increasing importance.

Land use planning as a policy instrument

2.5.25   The take up of passive solar and microclimatic design principles in the 'no regrets' and 'enhanced emissions reduction' scenarios, is unlikely to be achieved without the active involvement of the land use planning system. This would probably mean, at a minimum, planning policy guidance on how and to what extent these principles might be taken into account and may involve, as proposed by the Energy Committee, a requirement to consider them in relation to new development proposals. Planning guidelines might be a more flexible means of incorporating these principles than building regulations.

2.5.26   Active involvement of the planning system may help to ensure that the benefits of energy-conscious design are realised, but there will also be some costs. Additional construction costs are not inevitable, but may occur in some circumstances, for example, in order to achieve a high quality layout. Less tangible costs might also be incurred (for example, loss of amenity if a site chosen for microclimatic reasons is sub-optimal in other ways). Such costs would need to be considered in relation to individual developments and planning applications, but this is only likely to happen in any systematic way if there is appropriate guidance and/or a requirement to do so.

2.5.27   Using the land use planning system as a policy instrument would itself incur some costs, in terms of providing information, or implementing and administering new guidance or legislation. Developers *perceive* costs associated with energy-conscious design, and therefore at minimum there is an information cost in overcoming this perception. Peterborough District Council, for example, recently encountered 'strong resistance' from developers when it tried to encourage them to incorporate energy-conscious design principles in proposals for major new development.[185] As noted above, resistance might be smaller if land use planning policies were combined with other measures, such as the energy-labelling of buildings, which could help to make the market more transparent.

Wider implications

2.5.28   Like CHP/DH, energy-conscious design raises the issue of greater integration of land use and energy planning. In theory, land use planning could be a policy instrument to achieve built forms which were intrinsically more energy efficient (terraces and flats), to facilitate the introduction of CHP/DH (by higher density mixed development) and to realise the benefits of passive solar and microclimatic design. But the optimum urban structure for each of these may differ: terraces, for example, are intrinsically energy efficient but are the least flexible form for passive solar design.

2.5.29   If the mix of energy technologies (for supply and efficiency) could be optimised when development was planned, land use planning could then focus usefully on the most relevant criteria to influence. Where CHP/DH is not feasible, there could be greater emphasis on passive solar design, for example; and on urban infill sites where the latter is problematic, greater attention could be given to intrinsically efficient built forms. Some models are being developed for such optimisation techniques in Sweden[186], but it is an area which has received very little attention in the UK.

Research Needs

2.5.30   The most important research requirements in this area relate to the process of translating what is known in theory into design and planning practice.

2.5.31 Although there is consensus that passive solar and microclimatic design need involve no additional costs – implying that even with modest benefits there is a high benefit to cost ratio – resistance amongst developers and the slow diffusion of design principles imply that there *are* costs, or at least perceived costs, of some kind. These obstacles need to be better understood.

2.5.32 The full implications of including passive solar and microclimatic design principles in planning policy guidance and the respective roles of planning policies and building regulations in this context also merit exploration.

Summary

2.5.33 Energy-conscious design has the potential to make modest reductions in carbon dioxide emissions at little or no direct cost, and there is complementarity with other factors such as comfort both inside and outside buildings. However, there are many factors involved and significant information and institutional constraints. Under a 'business as usual' strategy, progress is likley to be relatively slow, but there are increasing pressures for at least a 'no regrets' strategy to be pursued. The level of implementation implied by an 'enhanced emissions reduction' strategy seems very unlikely for the foreseeable future.

2.5.34 There are strong links to land use planning because of the structural factors involved. While there appear to be no significant general conflicts with conventional planning considerations, such as daylighting and sunlighting criteria, it is important to take account of energy-conscious design requirements at an early stage and some changes to conventional thinking and practice may be required. The land use planning system is likely to be an instrument of any policies aimed at encouraging energy-conscious design.

2.5.35 Significant changes will only be effected in the long term. However, the potential for change is clearly much greater in areas where growth pressures are high, both because of the scale of new construction and because in areas of development pressure land use planners may have more leverage over factors such as design. These areas also tend to coincide with the areas of greatest potential for passive solar design.

2.5.36 Buildings usually last for many decades. Another way of looking at the time scale dimension is that if energy and environmental considerations are expected to become more significant in future, this presents an argument for *implementation* of the principles of energy-conscious design in the short term in order to maximise energy efficiency and minimise environmental impact in the medium to long term.

2.5.37 Research requirements relate to understanding the constraints on adoption of energy-conscious design and the costs and benefits of implementing appropriate land use planning policies. There is already a perceived need for policy guidance in this field.

2.6 Further Implications: Electricity Generation, Water and Recreation

2.6.1   In this chapter we consider several sectors in which developments have direct implications for land use planning, but where this interaction is less immediately or directly sensitive to climate change. We discuss, in turn, responses in the electricity supply industry (other than those already dealt with in Chapter 2.4).

ELECTRICITY GENERATION

The electricity supply industry and radiative forcing gas emissions

2.6.2   We have already noted that the electricity supply industry (ESI) is, and is likely to remain for some time, a significant source of rfg emissions (see Table 2 in Chapter 1.4), and will therefore be a focus for preventive policies.

2.6.3   Within the current regulatory framework, the ESI's response to such pressure will be to seek to maximise its output of electricity while minimising rfg emissions, though changes to this framework to encourage 'least cost planning'[187] might be envisaged in future. Options include:

- increasing the burn of low carbon-specific fossil fuels;

- increasing the burn non-fossil fuels such as wood or municipal and other wastes; and

- using non-combustion generation technologies, i.e. renewables such as wind power and also nuclear fission. These have minimal emissions of rfgs in operation.

2.6.4   Choices will be influenced to some extent by the NFFO, at present 98% met by purchases of

nuclear power, with the remaining 2% being mainly waste combustion.

2.6.5   Other options for reducing rfg emissions from this sector include improving the efficiency of primary energy use, introducing combined heat and power systems and 'end of pipe' pollution control technologies.

Relevance for land use planning

2.6.6   We have already considered the options with the most significant implications for land use planning – CHP, wind energy and tidal power – in Chapter 2.4. Here we draw together the implications of other possible responses in this sector. Land use planning sensitivities relate mainly to siting requirements and environmental impacts.

2.6.7   Some options, such as development of advanced coal generation technologies, could have significant local impacts (requiring sites on existing coalfields or near to the source of coal imports), but have only modest rfg abatement capacity[188] and seem unlikely to be pursued in the short to medium term. Similarly, flue gas decarbonisation[189] could have extensive infrastructure requirements but seems likely to remain uneconomic within the time-frame of the desk study. Some options, such as greater oil burn and the use of orimulsion, have minimal siting implications. Others seem likely to be adopted on only a relatively small scale, though there may be local opposition especially at sensitive sites. These include geothermal energy, generation from straw and stubble, livestock litter or fuel crops, and local hydro-electric power.

2.6.8 While noting the possible planning implications of some of these options, especially in the longer term, we do not consider them further in this chapter but focus instead on responses in the ESI which might impinge on the planning system in the short to medium term (or have significant development control implications). We consider fuel switching to gas, possible construction of further nuclear power stations, solar photovoltaic generation on buildings and the use of waste derived fuels.

Levels of response

2.6.9 The Department of Energy has considered a maximum potential implementation for different technologies in the ESI[190]. We have generally interpreted this as being the level attainable in an 'enhanced emissions reduction' strategy. At the other extreme, 'business as usual' is interpreted as a continuation of current trends. A 'no regrets' strategy tends to merge in this context with 'business as usual' because the main complementarities lie in contributions to emissions of other pollutants, such as acid gases, which are already the subject of quite stringent pollution controls.

2.6.10 We review in turn potential development of options (other than those considered in Chapter 2.4) which appear to have potential implications for land use planning. These relate mainly to site requirements and tend to vary in proportion to the capacity installed on a site for any given generation technology.

Fossil fuel 'switching' to gas

2.6.11 Emission rates of carbon dioxide from the combustion of different fossil fuels depend on the carbon/hydrogen ratio of the fuel. Comparison of this ratio for different fuels currently in widespread use clearly favours gas (Table 16). The efficiency with which heat energy can be converted to electricity increases in the direction coal – oil – gas. Overall relationships for state-of-the-art new build capacity are shown in Table 17.[191]

Table 16   Carbon dioxide emissions from electricity generation fuels

	mg carbon dioxide/kJ	% of coal emissions
Typical UK coal	88.4	100
Typical heavy fuel oil	72.6	82
Natural gas	50.2	57

Source: From figures prepared by ETSU.

Table 17   Carbon emissions from current and new generating systems

Plant Type	Efficiency (%)	10^6 tonnes carbon per Exa Joule electricity	Ratio of CO_2 produced to CO_2 from current UK power stations
Current coal fired	31.5	76.2	1
New coal fired	37.0	64.9	0.85
Modern combined cycle gas turbine*	42.0	33.3	0.44
Advanced combined cycle gas turbine*	47.0	29.8	0.39
Predicted combined cycle gas turbine*	50.0	28.0	0.37

*using natural gas.
Source: *Modern Power Systems*, April 1982; *Annual Review of Energy* 13,1988

2.6.12 In the absence of other constraints, there will be a strong preference in any ESI response to rfg emission reduction requirements for substitution of gas burn for coal. This fully complements other pressures which are stimulating increased gas burn in electricity generation, especially in the new circumstances of the electricity supply industry in the UK. These pressures include the requirement to reduce acid gas emissions, where gas has a very favourable profile, the low capital cost of combined cycle gas turbine (CCGT) plant and the relatively short lead times for plant construction.

2.6.13 Actual displacement rate of existing stock and increase in capacity from new-build CCGT will depend on a number of factors. These include the discovery rate of UK gas resources, the availability of external supply sources (and related considerations of national security), the ratio of natural gas prices to overall energy prices (and coal prices in particular) and the general level of these prices.

2.6.14 The industry consensus is that the next 10–12GW of generating capacity in the UK will be CCGT plant, both for replacement of decommissioned capacity and to meet growing demand. This pattern can therefore be taken as a 'business as usual' strategy. The 41GW by 2005 envisaged in EP58 could come about only under a very stringent 'enhanced emissions reduction' strategy in which there was unconstrained availability of natural gas at an acceptable price.

SITING AND LOCATION OF CCGT PLANT

2.6.15 The best available indication of the likely size of CCGT plant comes from data on proposed CCGT generation schemes.[192] These show that the range of individual schemes, proposed by both the existing power generation companies and private sector new entrants, is from 220MWe to 1725MWe, with a mean of around 700MWe.

2.6.16 Energy Paper 58's 'maximum' scenario of 41 GWe by 2,005 would imply the need for construction of around 60 mean-sized generating stations in the next 14 years, followed by a further 25 stations (17GW) in the subsequent 15 years. If the total 41GWe capacity were to be supplied by stations the size of the largest currently planned (the 1,725MWe Wilton station of Enron Power, on Teesside), this would require about 24 sites, whereas if the capacity were met entirely by the smallest of what seems currently to be regarded as economically viable (the 220MWe Roosecote station of Lakeland Power), something approaching 190 stations would be needed. It must be remembered, of course, that 41GWe represents an extreme scenario, based on giving very high priority to carbon dioxide emissions abatement.

2.6.17 Siting strategy will also be influenced by the comparative 'energy density' (GW/ha) of CCGT stations compared with the systems they are supplanting. National Power data suggest that CCGT plant have an energy density of 0.5GW/ha, compared with 0.2GW/ha for a modern coal-fired plant (with FGD). CCGT plant therefore have around a 2.5 times advantage in their land use requirements, largely because of the lack of need for fuel stocking areas.

2.6.18 All the indications are that new CCGT power stations built by the main post-privatisation generating companies would be either at sites of disused existing power stations (for example the Little Barford site of National Power)[193], sites already within the companies' land pool but where there are no existing stations (for example the Killingholme sites of both National Power and PowerGen) or at sites alongside existing power stations (for example National Power's Didcot station). CHP stations may be an exception to this, as discussed in Chapter 2.4.

2.6.19 There are very powerful incentives for new build plant to be on sites within the existing ownership of the generators. Technical factors include the advantages of an existing link into the National Grid system and the possible availability of common services shared with existing operational stations (for example cooling water treatment plant). There are also the 'property clawback' provisions of the Electricity Act which mean that until the end of March 2000, the UK Government will have a claim on the proceeds of land disposals by the privatised generators, except to a purchaser who continues the operational use of the property until the end of March

2000. These provisions will encourage the privatised generators to retain their existing operational land holdings and to dispose of them only for other power generation uses.

2.6.20 The locational pattern for 'new entrant' CCGT electricity generation is more diverse than for the CEGB successor companies. Some of the proposed schemes involve use of land formerly held by the CEGB. Others are associated with large existing industrial complexes, such as the Teesside project, at 1725 MWe the largest CCGT scheme yet put forward in the UK. This pattern is likely to be the norm for most 'new entrant' proposals. Green field site developments are unlikely to be common.

Nuclear power

2.6.21 Nuclear power stations emit no rfgs during operation and although some are produced in the fuel chain and construction of generating facilities, there is general agreement that, compared with fossil fuel electricity generation chains, nuclear power is favourably placed in respect of its impact on climate change. Eyre suggests that the nuclear generation option is an order of magnitude better placed than even CCGT in its total contribution to rfg emissions.[194] The primary issues which attach to the role that nuclear power could play in any rfg reduction strategies are other environmental impacts, relative cost effectiveness (in terms of cost per tonne of rfg abated) and the ability to construct stations on a demanding time schedule.

2.6.22 The current UK position is that future nuclear plant construction is 'on hold' until at least 1994, when a government review of the situation is scheduled. The only nuclear plant currently under construction in the UK—Sizewell 'B' is also scheduled to be commissioned in that year.

2.6.23 Energy Paper 58 has reviewed the possible contribution that nuclear power could make to rfg emission reduction in the UK. It argues that there is considerable scope for increasing nuclear power station construction, but identifies 'difficulties of obtaining planning permission' as one of the constraints considered to limit UK nuclear power station build to a maximum rate of two 1,175MW pressurised water reactors (PWRs) per year (less than half the rate achieved in France in the early 1980s). It also notes that actual future construction patterns might involve new designs of light water reactors (LWRs) rather than large PWRs but does not give further consideration to this possibility.

2.6.24 Energy Paper 58 developed scenarios based on a maximum build capability which would lead to a total installed PWR capacity of 8GW by 2005 (i.e. 6

additional Sizewell type PWRs, as well as Sizewell itself, and a further 40 similar stations by 2020). This was very much a speculative scenario and the full basis of the figures presented is not clear. Cases involving 25% and 50% of this maximum build scenario were also evaluated.

2.6.25 An accelerated PWR construction programme would most likely be constrained to involve exclusively existing sites where nuclear generation occurs, either those owned by Nuclear Electric, BNF plc (for example Chapelcross) or the UK Atomic Energy Authority (for example Winfrith). Technical considerations, primarily related to cooling water and grid connection availability and the current remote-siting safety policy would both combine to encourage this, as well as a marked industry preference for a 'nuclear park' approach because of its perceived consent-obtaining advantages. The Energy Paper 58 'full' and 50% PWR build scenarios by 2020 could well imply a need to opt for sites which are not currently linked to the nuclear fuel system. All indications are that this would be a major impediment to fulfilment of such scenarios.

Electricity generation from renewable sources

2.6.26 The Government has recently affirmed support for renewable energy technologies both for their diversity of supply (security) and environmental characteristics.[195] The White Paper on the Environment set a target of 1GW of renewable energy electricity generation by 2000. Wind and tidal power have already been considered in Chapter 2.4.

SOLAR PHOTOVOLTAIC ELECTRICITY GENERATION

2.6.27 A recent review of the prospects for solar photovoltaic technology (PV) in the UK over the period to 2025 concluded that PV is unlikely to make a significant contribution to UK electricity supply by that date[196]; installed capacity of about 200MW is projected. Remote systems (which might compete with local wind power or diesel generation) are economically attractive, but their contribution is limited by the size of the relevant markets, while central generating PV plants are unlikely to be competitive even under the most optimistic assumptions. However, distributed, grid connected systems mounted on buildings offer a number of potential advantages and, particularly when integrated into new commercial buildings, are identified as one of the main areas of interest for the UK in the longer term.

MUNICIPAL WASTE IN LANDFILL GAS AND DIRECT INCINERATION

2.6.28 Municipal waste in landfill sites decays, producing carbon dioxide and methane, along with other gases (for example CFCs, escaping from products containing them). Recent concern over the explosion hazard of methane leakage has led to an increasing number of schemes for draining methane from landfills. The methane may then be either flared direct to atmosphere, or used for heat or steam raising purposes including electricity generation. Such combustion of methane has the additional advantage of avoiding its direct radiative forcing potential if emitted uncombusted to the atmosphere and aso the rfg abatement from its displacement of the use of fossil fuels.

2.6.29 Although a proportion of municipal solid waste is of fossil-fuel origin, its combustion for generating electricity is regarded as non-fossil under the NFFO. This, and the increasing scarcity of sites available for landfill, are likely to increase the attractiveness of direct municipal waste incineration with electricity generation, although there is at present only one such scheme in operation, at Edmonton, north London. The contribution of this technology to rfg emission reductions is difficult to quantify. It avoids production of methane but the release of the carbon dioxide by combustion rather than decomposition gives a more rapid input to the atmosphere.

2.6.30 The likelihood of avoided costs from foregone landfilling rising (as transport costs to disposal sites and the costs of providing environmental protection at landfill sites escalate), together with the designation of municipal waste as a renewable source under the NFFO, will probably make municipal waste-fuelled electricity generation an attractive option without any additional incentives from rfg emission abatement. Although some schemes may involve water-borne transport to coastal sited incineration/ generation plant, modifying existing schemes for transport to landfill, there will probably be pressure for location of the necessary plant in urban or fringe urban areas with road transport of input fuel.

Land use planning implications

2.6.31 The main links between the options considered above and land use planning arise from land requirements and environmental impacts, both of which vary significantly between generating technologies. There do not appear to be major siting constraints for the options most likely to be adopted, though individual sites have the potential to be controversial in particular cases. With the possible exception of municipal waste incineration/ generation (see below), the land use planning system will mainly react to proposals for new generating capacity.

2.6.32 Two important time thresholds are the review of nuclear energy in 1994 and the anticipated expiry of the NFFO in 1998. Lead times for development of generating technologies range from short (for example CCGT, order of a few years) to potentially very long (for example, 10–15 years for a nuclear power station).

CCGT

2.6.33 The most significant change in the electricity generation sector is the increased preference for CCGT generation, which is occurring for reasons unconnected with any drive to reduce rfg emissions. However, the anticipated scale of development is unlikely to create significant issues for the land use planning system. There is likely to be an adequate supply of sites, certainly under the 'business as usual' scenario and probably also under a demand-only constrained maximum build scenario, as considered in Energy Paper 58. Nor is the land use planning system likely to be a major constraint on successful fulfilment of an accelerated programme of CCGT replanting.

2.6.34 This is not to suggest an absence of any local opposition to CCGT construction. This might be based on associated employment impacts, both directly and, more particularly, indirectly from the accelerated back-out from coal (1 GWe of CCGT generation requires 60 employees, compared with 275 for a new coal-fired plant[197]). Plans for a CCGT station at Staythorpe in Nottinghamshire have recently been opposed by the County Planning Authority on such grounds. The well known dereliction and infrastructural change issues from declining coal production might also be a significant, though indirect, planning-related issue from a CCGT replanting programme.

2.6.35 Opposition could also arise from the general reluctance of residents to host ANY form of industrial facility, although, as noted above, CCGT stations will mainly be built on sites which have hosted, or are already designated for, electricity generation. (CCGT stations for CHP may be exceptions to this, as discussed in Chapter 2.4). At least one new-entrant generation scheme for a green field site (a 380MWe CCGT at Rugby) has encountered local opposition to its development.

2.6.36 A major CCGT programme would probably lead to a surplus of land at current coal stations. There is no guarantee that the privatised generators will continue the former CEGB policy of preserving a large site portfolio, especially after March 2000 when the transitional 'clawback' arrangements for property disposals lapse. There may be land-use planning implications from the disposal of surplus land from generators. It is likely that the most suitable subsequent use for such land will be industrial development. Some sites within or on the fringes of urban areas could be attractive for other forms of development such as retail facilities. Redevelopment of all sites is likely to give rise to many of the well-known planning issues associated with major development, such as freight and personal transport and noise. An interesting point is that most, if not all, current power station sites are well served by rail connections for fuel supply purposes.

Nuclear power

2.6.37 It is difficult to discuss the implications of a significant nuclear power station construction programme in advance of the 1994 review, though pressure is building for an early reinstatement of the programme.[198] The planning system (through the special procedures adopted for power station consents) has had considerable experience of the issues involved in the recent past, including two of the most protracted and exhaustive inquiries in its history, in relation to applications for Sizewell 'B' and Hinkley Point 'C'.[199] Facilities for nuclear waste disposal have also been contentious. Whether the land use planning system would act as a significant constraint on any future nuclear power station construction programme is difficult to forecast. The industry is highly likely to opt for a standardised construction 'module' and to seek generic approval for major aspects of the chosen design. There would be pressure for the public inquiries to be restricted to site-specific considerations.[200]

2.6.38 If a preference were to develop for construction of smaller LWRs, the first such station proposed would most likely be exposed to a public inquiry examination at least as intense as that given Sizewell 'B'. Smaller LWRs might subsequently be to an extent freed from the siting constraints of larger stations. In theory, they ought to be as 'site mobile' as CCGT stations of similar size. In practice, it is difficult to conceive a situation where public apprehension about nuclear generation would be assuaged to such an extent that they could be sited with such freedom from constraint.

Other schemes

2.6.39 Municipal waste incineration/generation, possibly linked to CHP schemes (see Chapter 2.2), is the policy response most likely to create problems for the land use planning system in the short to medium term. Under present circumstances this can be viewed as a highly likely response to a rfg emission control strategy, especially one which included methane emission control in its remit. The planning system would need to accommodate the overall systemic co-ordination that the option involves.

2.6.40 The planning system's control of waste disposal schemes is well-developed. All indications are, however, that new landfill schemes are likely to become both more expensive and more difficult to progress through the planning system because of local opposition. Despite landfill gas heat/steam raising being incorporated into future proposals they are unlikely to be welcomed in a vicinity.

2.6.41 Waste-fuelled plant are likely to receive coniderable opposition to their location from local populations, related to issues such as alleged trace emissions from chlorinated substances in the input fuels in particular, as well as transport-related effects. Effective guidance on planning considerations related to municipal waste incineration schemes will be needed.

Research Needs

2.6.42 Few immediate research needs arise out of land use planning implications in this sector, but the following would merit investigation.

2.6.43 It would be useful for local planning authorities to compile an inventory of surplus sites which might arise from the switch away from coal based generation, though currently there are problems of uncertainty, political sensitivity and a relatively long time scale, perhaps two decades, over which such land might become available.

2.6.44 A more detailed assessment of the environmental and land use planning implications of municipal incineration/generation needs to be carried out since this is an option which seems likely to be pursued in the short-medium term.

Summary

2.6.45 The need to reduce rfg emissions from the electricity generating sector is unlikely to raise major issues of a general nature for the land use planning system, except in relation to CHP, wind and tidal power, which have already been considered. This is because the options most likely to be adopted can fairly readily be accommodated in terms of siting requirements.

2.6.46 Virtually no development is immune from local controversy, however, and siting for some options – such as generation from waste – is likely to be difficult.

WATER SUPPLY AND DEMAND
Introduction

2.6.47 The potential effects of climate change both on water supply and on water demand in the UK are extremely uncertain. In the case of summer precipitation, model results differ in direction as well as amounts, making analysis of the water supply implications very difficult.

2.6.48 The best estimates assume wetter winters and no change in precipitation, but greater evaporation and drier soils in warmer summers. The most important variable for the water industry is total effective rainfall (that is, the rainfall left after evaporation). An increased frequency of drought would be of considerable significance, but cannot be predicted from current models. We proceed in this chapter to consider the implications of the best estimates, with some sensitivity analysis where appropriate.

2.6.49 Climate change and sea level rise have a number of implications for the water industry. The most direct are the effects on surface and groundwater resources of changes in total effective rainfall and saline intrusion in coastal areas due to sea level rise; and the effects on water demand, especially peak demand, of warmer summers. Other implications include effects on water quality (for example, because of algal blooms or changes in agricultural practice). Parry and Read have summarised the sensitivities of the water industry to climatic variability (Table 18).

Relevance for land use planning

2.6.50 The most significant land use planning implications of climate change impacts on the water industry arise from requirements for new water supply infrastructure, particularly reservoirs.

2.6.51 In the face of rising demand, the land use and environmental implications of major developments related to water supply are already an issue in some areas, as is water abstraction from rivers, though this does not have direct land use planning implications. Climate change might make only a marginal difference in the short-medium term, but the possibility that it will exacerbate existing problems may serve to focus more attention on these issues.

2.6.52 A second, less direct and longer-term implication for land use planning could be envisaged if it becomes expensive to meet water demand in the South of the country, because of increased peak requirements and reduced effective rainfall. When critical thresholds could be foreseen, the benefits of further growth in some areas would need to be

Table 18 Impacts and sensitivities of climatic variability on the water industry's activities

Activity

Climate Effect	Water Resources	Water Treatment and Supply	Sewerage Treatment and Disposal	Pollution Control	Land Drainage	Sea Defences	Fisheries Conservation Recreation
Rain fall High	L/L	H-M/H-M water quality impaired; farm pollution; storm discharges; pipe bursts	H/H local operational problems	H-M/H-M water quality impaired; farm pollution; storm discharges	H/H flooding		
Drought	H/H related to time of year; duration; rain in previous period and location	H/H water quality impaired; high demand	M/M effluent dilution	H-M/H-M locally important			H/L water quality impaired
Snow High	L/L 'winter drought'	H/M site access affected; power failure	H/M local operational problems; site access; power failure		H/H flooding from snowmelt		
Temperature High	M/M increasd demand	L/L water quality impaired		M/M increased biological activity in rivers			H/M distress to fish stocks
Low (Frost)	L/L 'winter drought' (snow)	H/M-L local operational problems; power failure	H/L local operational problems			H/H surge and wave action	
Wind High	H/H security of dams	L/L local operational problems; power failure	L/L operational problems			H/H-M locally important	
Sea levels High	H-M/H-M saline intrusion; related to location and extent	H-M/H-M water quality impaired					

Key: Importance/cost   H=High, M=Medium, L=Low

Source: Parry and Read, 1988, reproduced in CCIRG, 1991 (see references).

weighed against the costs, both economic and environmental, of new water supply infrastructure. One effect of climate change might be to bring forward the date at which such thresholds will be encountered.

Current situation and forecasts

2.6.53 The National Rivers Authority (NRA) has published estimates of average demand for water supply undertakings to 2011 for all NRA regions and has compared these with actual resources and possible developments (Figure 17). (Resources and prospective demands to 2011 have also been assessed for each water undertaker).[201] The NRA points out that these statistics must be treated with considerable caution because it 'is only at the beginning of a process leading to a sustainable strategy for the management and development of water resources for England and Wales'.[202] However, the report provides a useful basis for a preliminary assessment of the land use planning implications of water industry responses to climate change.

2.6.54 The NRA's analysis suggests that average demand, as projected, will exceed existing resources before 2011 in five of the ten NRA Regions (Table 19).

Figure 17   Examples of NRA forecasts of water in relation to supply options

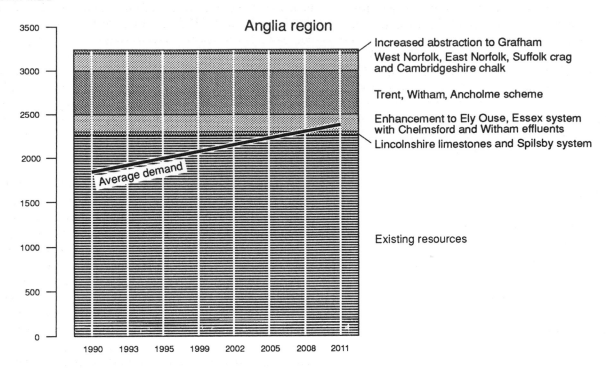

Units ML/D

Anglia region

- Increased abstraction to Grafham
- West Norfolk, East Norfolk, Suffolk crag and Cambridgeshire chalk
- Trent, Witham, Ancholme scheme
- Enhancement to Ely Ouse, Essex system with Chelmsford and Witham effluents
- Lincolnshire limestones and Spilsby system

Average demand

Existing resources

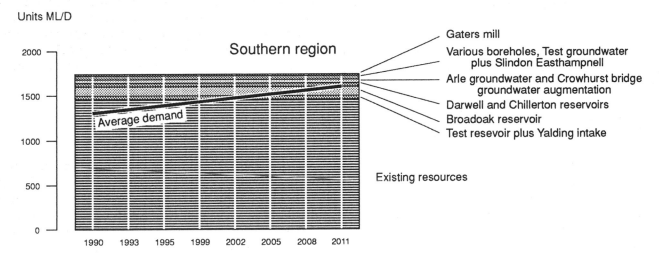

Units ML/D

Southern region

- Gaters mill
- Various boreholes, Test groundwater plus Slindon Easthampnell
- Arle groundwater and Crowhurst bridge groundwater augmentation
- Darwell and Chillerton reservoirs
- Broadoak reservoir
- Test resevoir plus Yalding intake

Average demand

Existing resources

Source : NRA 1991

Table 19   Adequacy of existing resources in NRA Regions

NRA Region	Date at which estimates suggest average demand will exceed existing resources
Anglian	2002
Severn Trent	1999
Southern	2002
Thames	1993
Wessex	2005

Source: NRA 1991

2.6.55   A number of qualifications must be taken into account when considering these figures. First, they reflect anticipated demand from water supply undertakers. Some industrial and agricultural operations abstract water directly (under licence from the NRA) and these abstractions may represent competing demands. (Demands for agriculture are expected to increase significantly). Second, since the NRA is currently in the process of auditing demand assessments, 'the values shown . . . should be viewed as a broad indication of possible trends.'[203] Third, the ratio of peak demand to average demand has implications for distribution infrastructure, a point to which we return below. Fourth, public water supply schemes are commonly designed for drought conditions. In Anglian and Thames regions, annual licenced abstraction is similar to or even exceeds the effective rainfall during severe droughts, which demonstrates the importance of water storage in reservoirs or as groundwater. Wetter winters, combined with higher demand for water resources in summer and possibly more frequent droughts would place even greater emphasis on storage.

Land use planning implications

2.6.56 As the Climate Change Impacts Review Group points out:

'In an industry where managing water has been based on past climate records, any change in climate may mean a mismatch between current design assumptions and the future environment. In some cases this will result in over-provision, but in many cases in under-provision'.[204]

2.6.57 Resource development options include reservoirs, pumped storage, direct surface water, river or groundwater abstraction, and surface water, groundwater or river augmentation. Of these it is primarily reservoir developments which have major land use planning implications, though other developments may have significant environmental impacts. Abstraction from rivers has both aesthetic and ecological implications, and abstraction from groundwater can have a detrimental effect on wetland ecosystems. Some developments are subject to Environmental Assessment (EA) even if they do not require planning permission. (For example, in Anglian region, increased abstraction to Grafham is listed as a possible development which would require EA.)

2.6.58 Reservoir developments are listed among the possibilities for Thames and Southern Regions (of the five regions where projected demand exceeds existing supply by 2011). Thames Water is already actively searching for a suitable site.

2.6.59 It seems unlikely that climate change impacts will significantly alter the slope of the demand curve or the availability of resource options before 2011. Land use planning implications in the short to medium term are therefore small. It must be stressed again that where reservoir developments are proposed, this is *already* a land use planning issue. The point is that the connection between water supply and land use planning is not very sensitive to climate change in the short to medium term.

2.6.60 In the longer term, land use planning implications may become more significant, but there are many uncertainties. Reservoir options may need to be considered more widely. Though not mentioned in the NRA Report, NRA Anglian Region's own recent report on future water resources discusses the possibility, on a timescale of 20 years or more, of climate change and a consequent 'strategic need for more large-scale storage'. The report argues that in this context a major new reservoir on the upper Stour could contribute to the needs of Thames Region as well as augmenting water resources throughout Southern Anglia.

2.6.61 There are also many more uncertainties, apart from those inherent in current climate change predictions, in the longer term. For example, there is likely to be increasing emphasis on demand management (such as water metering and leakage control) if the environment continues to be a matter for public concern. The major supply options – provision of reservoir capacity and surface and groundwater abstraction – all have negative environmental consequences and, as noted above, may be subject to increasing scrutiny through the EA system even when the land use planning system is not directly involved. If, in response to increasing environmental constraints and constraints on capital availability, a version of 'least cost planning' were to be adopted by the water industry the effects on the supply/demand balance might be much more significant than those of climate change.

Research needs

2.6.62 We have not identified any urgent research need in relation to land use planning. While in theory it should be possible to look further into the future and consider the potential impacts of climate change on both the demand and supply side (perhaps producing versions of the NRA's diagrams with longer time scales and a climate change factor), the uncertainties are so great that this might not at present produce useful results. Furthermore, reservoirs represent major, 'lumpy' investments involving lead times of at least 10–15 years. There is likely, in any case, to be quite considerable advance warning for the land use planning system of where and when they might be proposed as the most appropriate resource development option.

2.6.63 A study currently being funded by DoE at Leicester University will analyse past response of water consumption to climatic variation in the UK and examine the experience of countries with warmer climates. The results of this study may provide a useful basis for further exploration of land use planning sensitivities.

Summary

2.6.64 The land use planning implications of responses in the water sector arise mainly from the land take and environmental impacts associated with new infrastructure. These are not very sensitive to climate change at least in the short to medium term. If climate change exacerbates existing supply/demand imbalances, it may add impetus to the case for regional planning to direct development away from areas of greatest pressure on demand. While there is a need for a watching brief on climate-related developments in the water industry, we have not identified any immediate research requirements specifically connected to the land use planning implications of climate change in this area.

RECREATION AND TOURISM

Impacts of climate change

2.6.65 Tourism and recreation are likely to be sensitive to changes in climate both nationally and internationally.

2.6.66 The implications are, however, extremely uncertain. This is not only because of lack of knowledge about the details of climate change, but because tourism and recreation demand may be to a large extent supply-led. It is misleading to superimpose postulated weather patterns on *current* recreation and tourist activities.

Land use planning implications

2.6.67 It is nevertheless possible to postulate some effects of climate change on recreation and tourism which in turn have implications for land use planning. The main implications are for the balance between recreation and agriculture/forestry, especially in the uplands, for coastal recreational facilities and for access to areas where there may be increased fire risk. There may also be additional pressures on seaside resorts, with infrastructural implications and important effects on seasonal water demand.

2.6.68 The unpredictability of the British summer would not necessarily be reduced by climate change, but some studies predict an expansion of the UK tourist industry, especially for outdoor/activity styles of holidays. Farmers might be in a position to cap-italise on this trend and diversify their income base. Facilities provided would have planning implications, as would the possible need for new styles of recreation management. In National Parks, for example, the public have considerable freedom of movement in what is mostly an open grazed landscape. Climate change could create pressures for afforestation at higher altitudes and it could also become more economic to convert areas of pasture to arable crops.[205] If such changes occurred, the whole style of public access to national open spaces would be redefined.

2.6.69 Another significant issue for visitor management is that of increased fire risk in drier summers. Parts of Britain, such as the Dorset Heaths, already suffer severe fire problems. Currently destructive forest fires are a rare occurrence in the UK, but drier summers are likely to increase the risk. Most Forestry Commission forests are open to the public but a tangible increase in the risk of fire might have a negative effect on the already more limited public access to private woodlands.

2.6.70 Warmer, drier summers might lead to additional pressures on coasts and coastal resorts, adding to recreational management problems as well as those already associated with peak season demands, such as traffic congestion and water shortages. In areas susceptible to sea level rise, these pressures may be exacerbated, since they will be exerted upon a diminishing resource.

2.6.71 A potentially more immediate implication arises from ski-related developments, which are clearly climate related. Development proposals for ski facilities in Scotland have been controversial, primarily because of conflicts with nature conservation and other recreational interests. Anticipation that climate change could have an adverse impact on skiing potential in the medium term might be an additional material consideration in development control, but confidence in climate change predictions is probably inadequate to make such an argument at present.

2.6.72 Beyond these rather speculative considerations, it is difficult to identify more specific land use planning implications in any more detail. New opportunities may replace existing ones but it is premature to try to predict what these will be. We have not identified any immediate research needs in this area.

2.7 Agriculture, Forestry and Nature Conservation

Introduction

2.7.1 Agriculture, forestry and nature conservation are interrelated in a number of ways: agriculture and forestry may be alternative land uses, and both have major impacts on semi-natural habitats. During the course of the desk study, the land use planning implications of climate change were explored for each of these sectors using the analytical framework set out in Chapter 1.4. We also considered, as a separate policy response, afforestation as a means of carbon fixing. The overall conclusion, however, was that while the impacts of, and responses to, climate change in these sectors could have potentially profound effects on rural land use and the environment, there are few direct and immediate implications for the land use planning system.

2.7.2 The reasons for this are threefold. First, these are sectors in which the impacts of climate change, while potentially of great importance, are very uncertain and likely to have effect over long time scales. Second, in the short to medium term, other developments, such as reform of the Common Agricultural Policy (CAP) and loss of habitat due to development, will almost certainly be of greater significance. Third, the remit of the land use planning system in relation to agriculture, forestry and nature conservation is currently limited and the way in which its role might develop in future adds an additional element of uncertainty. One important impact of the high public profile of climate change may be to bring into sharper focus existing land use conflicts in these sectors.

2.7.3 We therefore consider these sectors in an integrated way and, rather than presenting the detailed analysis in each case, we first consider how climate change might impinge on agriculture, forestry and nature conservation in the UK, then focus on the most important overall conclusions relating to the land use planning system. Some interactions are shown in Figure 18.

Implications of climate change for agriculture, forestry and nature conservation

2.7.4 The implications of climate change for agriculture and forestry, and for semi-natural habitats in the UK have been explored in detail elsewhere and continue to be the subject of research.[206] The effects are complex and difficult to predict. Plant productivity is influenced by carbon dioxide concentrations, temperature, length of growing season and soil moisture levels. All of these parameters are likely to change. Other potentially important factors include the effects of soil moisture on the workability of the land, the impact of windthrow on trees and possible increases in pest populations. Semi-natural habitats are likely to be affected not only by climate change itself, through the spread or decline of different species and changes in community structure, but perhaps even more profoundly by responses in the agricultural and forestry sectors. Sea level rise is an additional factor.

2.7.5 Major uncertainties remain. Among the most important are the lack of quantitative information on winter and summer rainfall and on the frequency of extreme events; poor understanding of the response of crops and trees to environmental factors in field conditions; lack of knowledge of the critical climate parameters that may initiate the decline of forests;

Figure 18 Interactions between agriculture, forestry, nature conservation and land use planning

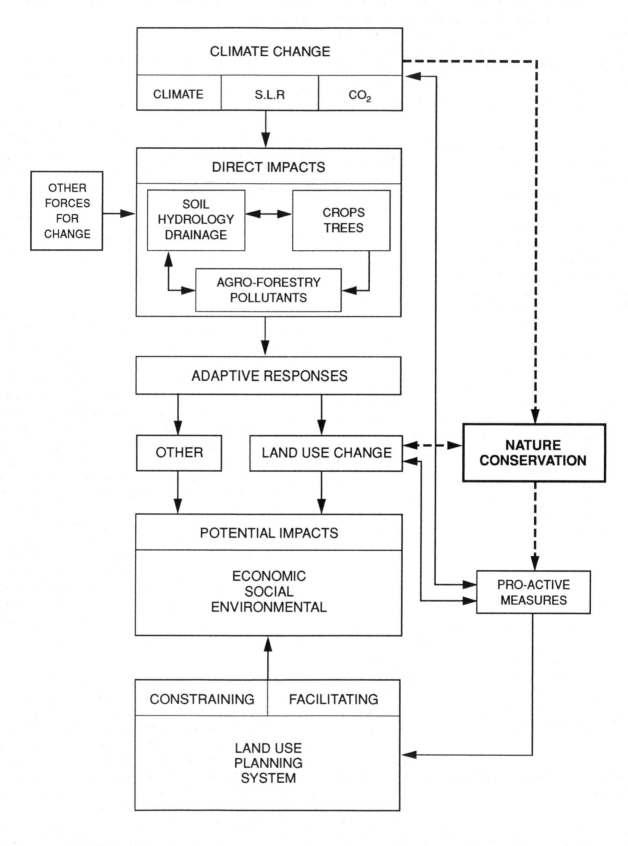

R. Cowell

and a relatively poor understanding of the ecology of pests, pathogens and weeds. In the case of agriculture (and forestry), the CCIRG conclude that information on climate change in the UK 'is currently insufficient for prediction of the full range of impacts'.[207] For semi-natural habitats it has been argued that, 'although we can expect bigger changes over the next 60 years than in any previous period of similar length, we are not in a position to predict them to any fine resolution'.[208]

2.7.6   If climate change occurs, some degree of adaptation will be necessary if farming and forestry enterprises are to survive. A 'status quo' strategy, in which farmers and foresters would seek to prevent reduction in yields while taking advantage of new opportunities, might involve greater use of fertilisers and pesticides, more irrigation, especially in the south and east of Britain and reappraisal of drainage needs. New management practices and new cultivars (such as drought resistant species) are also likely to be adopted. Many of these developments have implications for nature conservation.

2.7.7   An 'enhanced adaptive response' to climate change might involve more radical changes to crops and land use patterns. This might be envisaged in the longer term as new climatic patterns become established. The nature of any response remains highly speculative, but might include new crops (such as maize, soya beans, sunflowers and vines), shifts in existing crop zones (for example, a northward spread of grassland and a westward shift in the arable/pastoral line) and withdrawal from expensive-to-maintain soils (such as heavy clays and easily eroded sandy soils). At the same time, designations to protect habitats may need to be changed or extended.

2.7.8   In summary, climate change might lead to new agricultural and forestry practices, new crops and new land use pressures. Such changes have significant environmental implications both directly, for example through the use of agricultural chemicals and the demand for water, and indirectly through land use and landscape change and potential impacts, in addition to the direct effects of climate change itself, on the natural biota of the UK.

Afforestation and atmospheric carbon dioxide concentrations

2.7.9   Tree planting has long been promoted in the UK for a multiplicity of reasons. The perceived need to raise domestic timber output has been reinforced by (though has often been in conflict with) a strong amenity and conservation lobby promoting the planting of native broadleaved species. In 1988 there were nearly 2.3 million hectares of (mainly productive) woodland in Britain and the Government's target for new planting is 33,000 hectares per annum.[209]

2.7.10   Recently, the planting of trees as 'carbon sinks' has also attracted a considerable amount of attention.[210] The carbon fixing potential of afforestation is recognised in Environment White Paper[211] and it has been suggested that new forests would 'demonstrate the nation's commitment to the international effort to combat global warming'.[212] Though sequestration of carbon dioxide by trees is not permanent[213] and its realistic potential in the UK is relatively small[214], it may be seen as an acceptable way of 'buying time'. In May 1991, the Secretary of State for the Environment proposed that countries should include tree planting when estimating their impacts on the enhanced greenhouse effect.[215]

2.7.11   A number of schemes exist to provide an incentive for forestry, including the Woodland Grant Scheme, the Farm Woodland Scheme and the New Native Pinewood Scheme.[216] In addition, there are important new intiatives, led by the Countryside Commission, for Community Forests in the urban fringe of some 12 towns and cities in England, a new National Forest in the Midlands, and a Scottish Lowland Forest, planned for low grade agricultural and derelict industrial land between Edinburgh and Glasgow.[217] The diverse aims of these initiatives include amenity, nature conservation, timber production and the removal of surplus agricultural land. Though carbon fixing has not been a primary objective, the potential is significant. The Community and New National Forests could reasonably be expected to sequester 1.5tC per hectare per annum and the Scottish Lowland Forest some 45,000tC per annum, once established. A typical 15,000 hectare Community Forest might cost £25 million (including grants currently available).[218]

2.7.12   In an 'enhanced response' strategy, carbon fixing might become a more explicit objective of afforestation policy. The concept of 'carbon credits' could produce greater resources for Community and New National Forest initiatives, and financial support for other schemes could be increased. The possibility that the corporate sector might become more actively involved and provide a source of finance has already received some consideration, and one recent study concluded that the most cost-effective way for large corporations to fund carbon sinks in the UK would be to add funds to the National Forest scheme, or to give extra grants to upland farmers (supplementing the Woodland Grant Scheme) to allow natural regeneration of forest cover.[219]

Land use planning implications

2.7.13 In their assessment of the potential effects of climate change in the UK, the CCIRG argue that 'under changed climates there will be altered capabilities of using land for agriculture, recreation, conservation etc.' They conclude that attention needs to be given to land use planning policy: 'A national policy needs to be developed to consider how we should adapt to the transient changes in climate that are expected'.[220]

Current remit of the system

2.7.14 The problem, not discussed by CCIRG, is that the existing system of rural land use control is administratively and spatially fragmented, and the statutory planning and development control system currently has a limited remit in relation to agriculture, forestry and nature conservation. Though development control has recently been extended to cover the siting, design and external appearance of farm and forestry buildings[221], controls over agricultural and forestry operations are spatially restricted, largely of a voluntary nature and generally do not involve the land use planning system.[222] Similarly, while nature and landscape conservation may be the subject of development plan policies, are material considerations in development control and are the subject of forthcoming planning policy guidance[223], the remit of the land use planning system extends only to changes involving 'development' as defined by the Town and Country Planning legislation.

2.7.15 There are some exceptions to this generally limited remit, relating mainly to afforestation and to Environmental Assessment. In Scotland, for example, the Government has encouraged the Regional Councils to prepare 'Indicative Forestry Strategies', identifying 'preferred', 'potential' and 'sensitive' areas suitable for afforestation, and to include them in structure plans.[224] The new forest initiatives are also likely to involve the planning system: plans for the Community and New National Forests are intended to be compatible with, and reinforced by, those of local planning authorities.

2.7.16 Agricultural and forestry projects are currently included in Annex 2 of the European Community's Environmental Assessment (EA) Directive. EA is therefore discretionary and to date few farming or forestry projects have been called in for assessment. There is a possibility, however, that agricultural projects affecting semi-natural habitats and environmentally-significant forestry projects will be transferred to Annex 1, requiring mandatory EA. Such a move could add to pressures for more accessible consents procedures for such developments and could alter significantly the relationship between the land use planning system and the agriculture and forestry sectors. The necessary amendment is still 'pending'[225] but could be dealt with in 1993, when the EA Directive comes up for its five-year review.

Direct implications

2.7.17 Under the current system, however, the direct land use planning implications of responses to climate change in the agricultural and forestry sectors would largely be restricted to the need for new buildings, processing infrastructure and other development in response to changing production (and possibly rural population) patterns. It is too soon to predict such development pressures in any meaningful way, but they are unlikely to constitute the most significant impact of climate change on the countryside.

Implications of forest initiatives

2.7.18 Afforestation as a response to climate change only has implications for the land use planning system if it gives significant additional stimulus to existing schemes. These already involve the planning system to some extent, for example in recreational opportunities associated with increased tree planting and more active involvement in new major forest initiatives.

2.7.19 New forest initiatives have land use planning implications, manifest earlier and on a larger scale the greater the emphasis there is on tree planting. The relationship of the forest plan to those of the local planning authorities is intended to be one of negotiation and mutual adoption. Countryside Commission guidance suggests that the draft version of the forest plan should not conflict with other existing plans and strategies for the area (both statutory and non-statutory) and should aim to have the backing of all participants, including local authorities. The pre-plan survey should also aim to identify areas of high landscape or nature conservation value and incorporate them into the community forest.

2.7.20 There are implications for land use planning if the process of consultation involves not only the incorporation of all existing plans and planning permissions into the forest plan but also the reverse, with community forest policies being written into the new unitary and district development plans and regional policy guidance. It is possible to see the planning system developing an important information exchange and guidance role, keeping interested parties informed of the policy decisions of others. Planning for a future of climate change will need a detailed consideration of the long-term future plans of a number of organisations, and in the case of community forest plans, these considerations might be incorporated in the zoning of the forest area.[226]

2.7.21 Further land use planning implications arise if planning gain is employed as a strategy in the development of Community Forests. Developers could either be granted planning permission on the basis that the landowner may plant and/or manage a section of the Community Forest (for example, under Section 52 of the 1971 Act), or planning gain could be used as a means of acquiring suitable land, plus perhaps some funds for management, donated to the community forest scheme. Such a strategy is likely to be more successful in areas where the receipt of planning permission greatly boosts land values – the advice manual uses the example of Essex.[227] In some locations the land use planning system may be placed in a central position to increase the flow of funds and land to the community forest scheme. However, planning policy guidance suggests that the essential *principle* of planning gain 'is that the facilities to be provided or financed should be directly related to the development in question or the use of land after development'.[228] It remains to be seen whether tree planting schemes could meet the criteria set out in the guidance (which is currently under revision).

2.7.22 The possibility that planning permission might be granted for development in protected areas such as green belts in return for sizeable contributions to the Community Forest project is already causing some concern amongst amenity and conservation groups. CPRE, for example, have called for planning guidance relating to Community Forests, including the need for planning permission for significant afforestation, for Environmental Assessment of each Forest Proposal and for control of the scale and speed with which Community Forests are being promoted.[229]

Implications in relation to nature conservation

2.7.23 In relation to nature conservation, a minimal response of the land use planning system would be to participate in a much more comprehensive system of ecological and environmental monitoring, which could provide the basis for an informed response to climate change as evidence becomes available about likely impacts. Lack of baseline data 'is proving to be a stumbling block to making informed predictions of semi-natural community change in the next half-century'.[230] Such a monitoring system is desirable in any case, since many other changes threaten natural and semi-natual habitats, and the threat of climate change may provide an additional stimulus. This could perhaps be co-ordinated with the European Community's CORINE database.

2.7.24 Another possible response would be for the planning system to afford greater priority to nature conservation in land use conflicts, for example through a strong presumption against loss of or damage to sites of international or national importance. (Maps are available to all local planning authorities showing notified nature reserves in their area). The rationale for this would be two-fold. First, since precise impacts are unknown but it cannot be guaranteed that climate change will result in net benefits to nature conservation, there is logic, particularly in the short term before more information becomes available, in adopting a 'precautionary principle' to maximise the chance of maintaining valued interests in future. Like all insurance policies, this strategy would have costs, but it would also have immediate benefits for conservation: both would be very difficult to quantify.

2.7.25 A second argument for placing greater emphasis on conservation now would be to preserve as wide a range of sites as possible to keep open the option of transference in future, should this prove to be the only way to preserve particular species or systems. Criteria for nature conservation include the need to be representative of the diversity of ecological, edaphic and climatic variation in the UK.[231] If a diverse, representative range existed, then at least there might exist a suitable habitat to transfer species or ecosystems to. This is an unproven strategy, however, for it is likely that the different component parts of ecosystems would react in different ways to climate change and the overall result would be new assemblages, not the same ecosystems in different place.[232]

2.7.26 Land use planning might also have a role, within its current remit, in facilitating the migration of ecosystems, particularly in the coastal zone. Migration of coastal ecosystems may be prevented by hard defences, roads or urban development; there is therefore a role for the planning system, in co-operation with other bodies, in deciding which systems might be particularly important and mobile (there are some 180 coastal notified nature reserves of at least national importance[233]), and in exercising development control in the hinterland so that they are not prevented from moving. A precedent for such policies exists in Maine, in the US, where consent is granted for development landward of important coastal ecosystems (such as wetlands and dune systems) on condition that development will be removed if it prevents the natural migration of such systems.[234]

2.7.27 More generally, any change or extension of designations to protect habitat in response to changing ecological conditions or newly-emerging land use pressures would need to be taken into account by land use planning authorities. This is a potentially important implication, but it is not possible in the current state of knowledge to define it in locationally-specific terms.

Wider implications for the land use planning system

2.7.28 Over the relatively long timescales which we are considering, however, greater co-ordination of policies affecting rural land use might be achieved. Perhaps the most significant implication for land use planning in relation to agriculture, forestry and nature conservation is the possibility that the threat of climate change might itself be an important stimulus to such co-ordination.

2.7.29 One effect of climate change would be to modify the geography of opportunity cost, perhaps very significantly. This change might be greatest in the north and uplands of Britain, where a combination of latitude and altitude make farming an economically marginal land use at present, with little incentive to invest in land improvements. This could change markedly if the climate of Britain warms during the next century. Similarly, climate change might encourage the production of lucrative but environmentally undesirable crops (for example, the growth of vines on erosion prone soils). In all cases where economic incentives are in place to deter an undesirable land use, the level of that incentive will need to be reviewed as opportunity costs change. It may become increasingly costly to prevent intensification in areas of high conservation value and more difficult for a system of financial incentives to produce desirable outcomes without being backed by overarching spatial guidelines for the countryside. Some observers have argued for a strategic plan to provide a coherent framework for British agriculture in a period of rapid change.[235]

2.7.30 If carbon fixing becomes a more explicit objective of afforestation, there are also implications for rural land use planning seen in its wider context. For example, there are potential conflicts with amenity and conservation.[236] A recent report suggests that planting more conifers on marginal land in the uplands would probably be the most cost effective way of increasing carbon stores in the UK, though there is much debate about the carbon fixing potential of conifers versus broadleaves.[237] Improving the productivity of existing forests could also enhance their carbon dioxide assimilation rates.[238] This implies maximising stocking densities, growing only very productive tree species, and adding fertilizers – all the features of a modern plantation. Conflict over afforestation is not new but it has to date been between economic and amenity/conservation objectives and has been an important factor behind pressure for greater involvement of the planning system in rural land use change. This may be another area, therefore, where the threat of climate change focuses renewed attention on an issue with which the land use planning system is already familiar.

2.7.31 It is also significant that whilst on most soils, changing land use to trees would add to the net carbon store, or at least make very little difference, the afforestation of unflushed peatland soils is a distinct exception. Since the establishment of a tree crop on peat inevitably involves lowering the water table (both by drainage before planting, and by evapotranspiration) and consequenty a greater aeration of the peat, that aerobic layer starts to decompose faster and release its store of carbon. A significant proportion of the land afforested over the last two decades may in fact be resulting in a net flux of carbon to the atmosphere.[239] This suggests that Forest Indicative Strategies, with which land use planning authorities are involved, need to take into account edaphic factors that affect the net carbon flux.

2.7.32 All of the above considerations might reinforce the case to take a more holistic view of the pressures and constraints on rural land use to form a more comprehensive spatial strategy. As understanding of the impacts of climate change developed, such a framework would be in a better position to take them on board than the current fragmented system. For example, the futures of the farming and forestry sectors and that of the water supply industry are interconnected in many ways, and the future development of both might be usefully coordinated, at least in some regions.[240] Areas suitable for particular kinds of agriculture and forestry, as well as areas requiring special protection, for example from soil erosion, could be identified. The needs of nature conservation would be an integral part of this system and the more holistic approach could make it easier to take on board the modified requirements for nature protection in a period of rapid climatic change. For example, it might help to preserve the geographical integrity of the extensive areas of semi-natural habitats in the uplands or to maintain and create links between lowland habitats. This would involve the land use planning system and well as other agencies in what would effectively amount to rural land use planning. Such policies have always been resisted to date but climate change in combination with other major reforms affecting the rural environment might provide sufficient stimulus for action.

Research Needs

2.7.33 Research needs relate mainly to the long term, though in some cases results would be useful regardless of whether climate change takes place. We have identified the following potentially useful studies:

- analysis of the criteria for designation of protected areas. What are the fundamental elements which we seek to protect? How might these be affected by climate change? This could be a 'thought piece' on environmental philosophy, drawing on existing work and/or a survey of what designations actually mean to those involved;

- a study of the efficiency of financial incentives and planning control in guiding rural land use change. There is already a body of literature on this which could usefully be collated and synthesised, and which may need updating in the light of recent changes to the CAP. An economic framework would be useful, but 'efficiency' should not be too narrowly defined. The results of such work would inform the current debate but would be particularly valuable if the geography of opportunity costs change significantly under the influence of climatic factors;

- analysis of the potential for integration of different policies influencing the development of rural land use. Environmentally sensitive areas (ESAs) would provide one starting point and various proposals for reform of the CAP[241] another, but the study should aim to explore the potential to integrate land use planning with other policies, and to identify the main costs and benefits of doing so. It could be based on one or more case studies in different kinds of rural area;

- further work on the amenity/conservation value of forests; this would be of value in any case, but may become more important if planting for carbon fixing potential conflicts with amenity;

- a desk study of the options for landward migration of coastal ecosystems; this could cover experience elsewhere; planning policy options; costs and benefits; and criteria for selection of ecosystems to merit this special treatment; and

- the interaction between agriculture, forestry, water, conservation and urban development needs to be analysed, possibly with the aid of case studies in specific geographical areas, with the aim of developing a systems model of the interaction into which climate change parameters, as they became better known, could be fitted.

Summary

2.7.34   Climate change will be only one of many influences on the agriculture, forestry and nature conservation sectors over the next few decades and there are already strong pressures for reform of agricultural policy. The primacy of agricultural land has already been reduced (for example, DoE Circular 16/87 reduces the priority given to the quality of agricultural land in development control decisions). The level of response to climate change must depend, to a large extent, on the actual physical manifestation of impacts, and is unlikely to have significant implications for the land use planning system in the short to medium term. The most important effect, as with many of the sectors where we consider adaptive responses, may be to provide an extra stimulus to a wider debate about rural land use change. Co-ordination of the many policies affecting rural land use would have major implications for the land use planning system.

2.7.35   Climate change has profound implications for land use. Its implications for land use *planning* depend on whether the currently limited remit of the statutory land use planning system in relation to the agricultural and forestry sectors is maintained or a more co-ordinated system of rural land use management is developed. Climate change might add to the stimulus for such development because of the changing geography of opportunity costs and the interactive nature of many potential responses to climate change in the agriculture, forestry, water and nature conservation sectors. In such a situation, the land use planning system could play an important part in delineating broad areas suitable for different land uses.

2.7.36   In the short term, the review of the Environmental Assessment Directive in 1993 is significant, since it may result in the transfer of some agricultural and forestry operations to Annex 1, with possible implications for consents systems. Otherwise, the relevant timescales are really set by climate change itself. Significant changes and responses in the agricultural and forestry sectors are very unlikely in the short term and other factors, especially developments in the CAP, will dominate (though these may raise many similar issues to climate change). A rural land use strategy developed over the medium term (say 10–15 years) might provide a better basis than the currently fragmented system for coping with the problems and opportunities associated with climate change, if and when they manifest themselves. The land use planning system must be mainly reactive to agriculture and forestry proposals, and then only in a limited sense, in the short term, though there is some indication of more proactive involvement (for example Scottish

Forest Indicative Strategies). In the longer term, land use planning might play a key role in integrated rural development.

2.7.37　Research needs include analysis of criteria for designation of protected areas; a study of evidence about the efficiency of financial incentives and planning control in guiding rural land use change; analysis of the potential for integration of different policies influencing the development of rural land use and identification of the costs and benefits of integrating land use planning with other policies. More generally, the interaction between agriculture, forestry, water, conservation and urban development needs to be analysed in some detail.

Conclusions and Priorities For Further Research

3.1   Conclusions

3.2   Priorities for further research

3.1 Conclusions

3.1.1 The desk study covered a very diverse range of possible land use planning implications arising from climate change. Detailed conclusions relevant to particular physical impacts and adaptive and preventive responses are to be found in the individual chapters in Part 2 of this report. Here we draw together the more general conclusions which emerge from the study as a whole.

The need to consider land use planning implications of climate change

3.1.2 The land use planning system by definition deals with the future and is therefore accustomed to the problems of decision making under uncertainty. In the case of climate change, as we have stressed throughout this report, these problems are manifest in an acute form. The nature and timing of impacts for an area as small as the UK cannot yet be predicted with any confidence and uncertainty is unlikely to be much reduced for 15–20 years. Best current estimates indicate warmer (and more extreme warm) summers with drier soils and warmer, wetter winters by the middle of the next century, with sea levels about 30cms higher than today. Additional major uncertainties attach to policy responses to these impacts and to social and technical change over the relatively long time periods involved.

3.1.3 It might therefore seem premature to consider the land use planning implications of climate-induced environmental change and policy responses to it. However, there are at least three reasons for beginning this analysis now. First, it is possible to make an initial assessment of the *sensitivities* of the planning system to future changes and policies and to identify areas where attention might most usefully be focused. Second, any necessary adaptations on the part of the planning system itself may only be effective over long timescales and may need to be initiated within the next few years. Finally, the system may need to be in a position to react quickly if physical change and political responses occur suddenly and unpredictably, rather than along a smooth curve.

Priorities for the planning system: the sectoral analysis

3.1.4 Not all potential responses to climate change have identifiable land use planning implications. We selected a number of areas where physical impacts and preventive or adaptive policy responses might impinge directly or indirectly on the land use planning system. The significance of the interaction was judged according to the likelihood of such an impact or response occurring (and the timescale over which this might happen) and the strength of the link with land use planning.

3.1.5 According to these criteria, the most important land use planning implications of climate change arise from the impacts of sea level rise and adaptive policy responses to the increased threat of flooding and erosion in the coastal zone; and from policies which might be adopted to reduce emissions of rfgs in the transport sector. In both cases, responses can be envisaged in some scenarios in the short to medium term and land use planning has both a reactive and a potentially significant proactive role. There is a need for further theoretical and empirical research and for policy guidance in the near future.

3.1.6   Other areas with potentially significant land use planning implications relate to energy supply and demand in the built environment and further development of some of the more promising renewable energy sources. We include the further development of urban-scale CHP, passive solar and microclimatic design of buildings, on-shore wind energy and tidal power. While the likelihood of extensive development is only modest in the most realistic scenarios, the links with land use planning are relatively strong in each case. Information, monitoring, further research and some planning policy guidance will be required.

3.1.7   Other impacts and responses which might impinge on the land use planning system can be identified in the electricity supply and water industries, in recreation and tourism, in agriculture and forestry and in nature conservation. For various reasons – for example, great uncertainty, long timescales or a relatively weak link with land use planning – these implications are less immediate and/or less direct than those mentioned above. This does not imply that the links are unimportant or that they do not merit some attention now. However, in these cases the need for a short term response on the part of the planning system was not demonstrated by the desk study.

Thematic conclusions: land use, development pressures and the role of the planning system

3.1.8   If we take a thematic, rather than a sectoral, view of the land use planning implications of climate change, some significant general implications emerge in terms of land requirements, redistribution of development pressures, the role of land use planning as a policy instrument and the remit of land use planning in relation to other policies.

Land requirements

3.1.9   None of the preventive or adaptive responses to climate change has major implications for the land use planning system in terms of significant direct land requirements in the short to medium term. However, wind power, though unlikely to be implemented extensively on this timescale, raises novel and potentially controversial siting issues. Net land take is small, but wind farms preclude many other land uses over large areas. A number of proposals are likely to come before the land use planning system and because of the issues that they raise in terms of land take and landscape impact, local planning authorities will require some guidance in dealing with them. (Guidance on renewable energy and the planning system is forthcoming[242]).

3.1.10   Other electricity generation options tend to have lower specific land requirements than the energy sources which they are replacing, though virtually all developments are potentially controversial. Nuclear power stations and refuse incineration schemes are very likely to be contentious as are any developments using green field sites, though the latter seem likely to be relatively small in number.

3.1.11   An accelerated shift away from coal-based energy, possibly brought about by fiscal measures such as a carbon tax, is an increasingly likely response to climate change. Coal as a source of energy has required large amounts of land, for example for coal stocking yards, not required by the sources which may substitute for it, such as gas. This land may therefore become surplus to requirements. Further decline of coal mining will contribute to surplus, often derelict, land. Sites could be reclaimed and used for some other, possibly industrial purpose, but decontamination may be necessary.

Redistribution of development pressures

3.1.12   In some cases, responses to climate change could lead to a significant redistribution of development pressures. These are most likely to arise from modified travel patterns, planned or unplanned retreat in the coastal zone and the changing geography of opportunities in the agricultural and forestry sectors. While these implications are far from certain, and are only likely to manifest themselves in the medium to long term, they are important because they are potentially of considerable significance for patterns of land use and because the land use planning system itself requires relatively long timescales in which to adjust to new pressures, unless it is to be entirely reactive. These new pressures also have implications for the scale at which the land use planning system operates.

Land use planning as a policy instrument

3.1.13   In a number of the sectors examined, the most important land use planning implication is that the planning system itself may be used as a policy instrument. Most significantly, it could contribute to improved efficiency of energy use in the built environment at all scales (Figure 19); and it could play a key role in an adaptive response to increased flood and erosion hazards in the context of integrated coastal zone management. The potential is increasingly acknowledged in both cases, but the costs and benefits of involving the land use planning system in this way have never been very clearly defined. This is a key area for further research[243].

Figure 19   Factors affecting energy demand at different scales of development

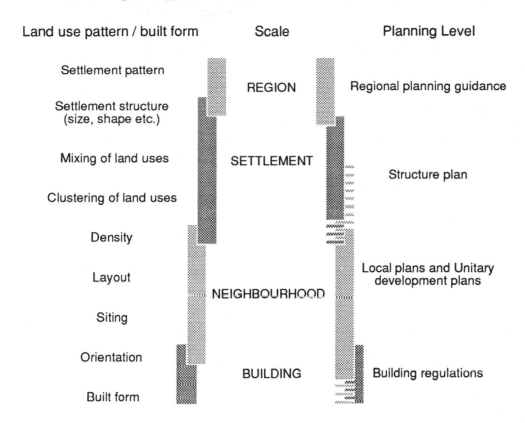

Source : Owens 1991

3.1.14   An important conclusion is that land use planning as a policy instrument is unlikely to be effective if it is working in isolation, 'against the grain'. For example, location policies which seek to influence travel behaviour may have counterintuitive effects unless combined with fiscal policies which convey essentially the same message to energy consumers.

Climate change as a stimulus to reform

3.1.15   An important finding of the desk study is that climate change can focus attention on existing problems and may give new impetus to pressures for policy reform. Particularly in sectors where the remit of the planning system is currently limited, such an effect may be the most significant land use planning implication of climate charge.

3.1.16   Greater co-ordination and rationalisation of policies influencing rural land use change, nature conservation and the coastal zone have long been urged, especially by environmental interests, quite independently of climate change. But if climate change provides a vehicle for reform, the remit of land use planning may be significantly extended in these areas.

3.1.17   Pressures for greater integration of land use and energy supply planning are likely to arise in 'no regrets' and 'enhanced emissions reduction' scenarios, particularly in relation to energy supply options which have significant urban structural implications, such as urban-scale CHP and passive solar energy. The planning system may need new powers in order to respond to these pressures.

3.1.18   Water supply constraints in the medium to long term under some climate change scenarios may mean that restraints on growth need to be considered as an option in some areas. Though this effect remains very uncertain on the basis of current information, it could add to pressures for a regional level of land use planning.

3.2 Priorities for Further Research

3.2.1   Research needs were identified in each of the sectors examined in the desk study and are outlined in each chapter of Section 2. Here we summarise the more general research requirements emerging from the study, often related to more than one sector.

3.2.2   Exploration of the land use planning implications of climate change is at an early stage and not surprisingly it is possible to identify many areas where further research is required. It is useful to consider these requirements in several categories, though not all are mutually exclusive.

Basic research

3.2.3   There is clearly a need for basic research, both theoretical and empirical, to improve our understanding of interactions between responses to climate change, patterns of land use and land use planning policies. Examples include the need for further modelling of the energy and environmental implications of urban and regional development patterns; assessment of the infrastructure, land and siting requirements associated with transport policies, such as those aimed at modal shift; and more detailed spatial or sectoral analyses of infrastructure at risk from flooding and erosion.

3.2.4   Some research falling into the basic category is essentially of a philosophical nature. For example, a critical analysis of criteria for designated areas of all kinds, and consideration of the fundamental elements which society seeks to protect, would provide a grounding for land use planning and related policies in a period of rapid environmental and ecological change.

Costs and benefits of land use planning policies

3.2.5   In theory at least, responses to climate change should be prioritised according to their costs in relation to the benefits delivered. Some attempts are being made to do this (see Chapter 1.4), but it seems that none has included the land use planning system in any quantified analysis. Possibly this is because it is simply too difficult to do (there seems to be little work on the 'costs' of the planning system more generally), but it is clear that land use planning involves both costs and benefits and it would be useful to develop a conceptual framework for such an analysis even where quantification is not possible.

3.2.6   Such analyses will be particularly important in relation to transport, coastal zone management, energy-conscious design and rural land use planning, where the planning system might be employed as an instrument of preventive or adaptive policy in relation to climate change. Costs and benefits need to be compared, at least in qualitative terms, with those of other policies (such as fuel switching, building regulations, fiscal measures or improving sea defences). It is also important to understand the relationship between different kinds of policies, for example whether location policies and fiscal policies in the transport sector are alternatives, complementary or additive in their impact on travel demand.

Empirical 'groundwork' studies

3.2.7   In a number of areas there is a clear need for monitoring to assess current practice and to identify constraints in relation to possible policy change. For example, many local planning authorities are already adopting policies with climate change as a justification; these include location and transport policies considered to be 'energy efficient' and development control policies in coastal hazard zones. A survey of planning authorities and existing land use and transport policies to define the extent of this response would serve a number of purposes: it could highlight complementarity with other objectives, and constraints; it could provide useful information about adoption rates and likely effectiveness of such policies in the absence of central government guidance; and it could show how any forthcoming guidance could most effectively be formulated.

3.2.8   Other areas where assessment of experience and constraints would be particularly revealing include development of CHP, promotion of energy-conscious design, experience with forest initiatives and enforcement of existing policies relating to flood hazard zones.

International comparative work

3.2.9   Experience and constraints in other countries can also provide valuable lessons, providing that sufficient account is taken of cultural, economic and political differences. For example, reference is often made to better integration of land use planning with the planning of energy supply and conservation in other countries, such as Denmark and Sweden, but the institutional context is very different from that of the UK. A comparative study is needed, to define the extent to which good practice could be transferred with or without institutional change, the kinds of change which might be needed, and how realistic it is for the UK. Comparative work on transport policies, for example on the cultural and institutional factors which influence the acceptability of transport policies in different countries, would also be useful. A desk study of the options for landward migration of coastal ecosystems would also fall into this category, drawing on experience elsewhere and possibilities in the UK to identify planning policy options, costs and benefits, and criteria for selection of ecosystems to merit this special treatment.

Work on system interaction

3.2.10   Analysis of the land use planning implications of responses to climate change highlights the strongly interrelated nature of potential impacts and responses in a number of sectors. There are some difficulties in analysing separately possible developments in agriculture, forestry, water supply and demand, nature conservation, the coastal zone and the tourism/recreation sector. A systems model of the interactions among these sectors would provide a better basis for further analysis of land use planning implications. An initial task might be to develop such a model conceptually; if successful, it might then be applied to examine the sensitivity of the system to changes in climatic and other variables.

Development of analytical tools

3.2.11   There is a need for continued development of analytical tools and methodologies for both research and policy development. For example, local planning authorities will need means of assessing the energy and environmental implications of plans and policies, and there is a need to translate results of more fundamental research into methods suitable for application at this level. Where uncertainty is a very significant feature of an issue, decision analysis may provide a useful framework for policy choices and for determining the value of information. Elaboration of decision analysis frameworks, for example in relation to development control in coastal hazard zones, would be a worthwhile exercise. Some responses to climate change may provide excellent test cases for further development, improvement and testing of existing but often controversial techniques such as environmental assessment, landscape evaluation and contingent evaluation: proposals for wind farms, tidal barrages or municipal incineration/generation facilities, for example, clearly provide such opportunities.

The need for planning policy guidance

3.2.12   We have stressed throughout this report that many of the issues raised by climate change for the planning system are not new. But climate change modifies the context within which the planning system operates. It will demand a response, or at least a new level of awareness, in a number of areas in which the planning system traditionally operates and in some cases may encourage an extension of the system's remit.

3.2.13   In some areas relevant to climate change the need for planning policy guidance (PPG) is already apparent. PPG notes are expected on renewable energy development, nature conservation, coastal zone management and reducing the need to travel through land use planning policies.[243] Guidance on energy-conscious design may be forthcoming[244], and some guidance might also become desirable on issues related to CHP. Though in many cases guidance is stimulated by other considerations, it is important that both existing and planned PPGs take account of new issues raised by climate change and that it should be updated where necessary as uncertainties are reduced.

3.2.14   In the cases of some of the issues considered in this report, planning policy guidance would not yet be appropriate. Some of the land use planning implications of climate change are so uncertain, long term or indirect that all that can be recommended for the present is that the planning system maintains a 'watching brief' in these areas. Much remains to be done, but we hope that this initial exploration of the land use planning implications of climate change has identified key areas for policy action, further research and monitoring, and that it will stimulate debate about a potentially profound influence on the land use planning system in future.

Notes and References

1 Houghton, J. T., Jenkins, G. T. and Ephraumus, J. J. (eds) (1990) *Climate Change: The IPCC Scientific Assessment*, Report of Working Group I, Intergovernmental Panel on Climate Change, Cambridge, Cambridge University Press.

2 Land use planning in England and Wales is a two-tier system. County planning authorities are responsible for the preparation of structure plans covering broad land use issues. Within this framework district planning authorities prepare local plans and are responsible for development control. Following abolition of the metropolitan counties in 1986, the metropolitan boroughs are responsible for the preparation of unitary development plans and for development control. The two national park planning boards in England are also development control authorities. There is no statutory regional planning system, but the Department of the Environment has begun to issue regional planning guidance based broadly on the advice prepared by local authorities who are grouping together to form regional planning conferences. The Department also produces a series of planning policy guidance notes (PPGs) on specific issues, such as housing or the content of structure plans, which set out Government policy on key issues. In Scotland, the system differs in a number of ways, for example the upper tier of land use planning is the responsibility of the Regional Councils.

3 An interesting exception in the UK is the work of the London Boroughs Association (LBA) who discuss planning implications extensively in their report LBA (1991) *Global Warming: the Implications for London* London, LBA.

4 UK Climate Change Impacts Review Group (CCIRG) (1991) *The Potential Effects of Climate Change in the United Kingdom*, First Report for the Department of the Environment, London, HMSO.

5 Barker, T.(ed) (1991) *Green Futures for Economic Growth*, Cambridge Econometrics.

6 CCIRG, 1991, *op. cit.*

7 Houghton, J. T., Jenkins, G. T. and Ephraumus, J. J. (eds) (1990), *op. cit.*

8 GCM is also used as an acronym for global circulation models.

9 Houghton, J. T. *et al, op. cit.*

10 Dr. Bennetts, Hadley Centre, pers. comm. 1991.

11 Hadley Centre (1990) *First Report of the Research Co-ordinator*, Meteorological Office, September.

12 Dr. Bennetts, Hadley Centre, pers. comm. 1991.

13 Secretary of State for the Environment *et al* (1990) *This Common Inheritance: Britain's Environmental Strategy*, Cm 1200, London, HMSO.

14 Through events such as the 1985 UNEP, ICSU and WMO International Conference on the Assessment of the Role of Carbon Dioxide and Other Greenhouse Gases in Climate Variations and Associated Impacts, held at Villach, Austria.

15 Rt. Hon. M. Thatcher, speech at opening of Hadley Centre.

16 Secretary of State for the Environment *et al, op. cit.*

17 *Financial Times*, 26.6.91.

18 Council of the European Communities (1990) *Minutes of the 1436th Meeting of the Council (Joint Energy/Environment Council), 9612/90, Brussels, 9/11/90.*

19 Commission of the European Communities Draft Communication to the Council on *A Community Strategy to Limit Carbon Dioxide Emissions and to Improve Energy Efficiency*, Brussels, DG XI, 15.5.91.

20 Council of the European Communities (1990) *op. cit.*

21 Commission of the European Communities (1991) *Proposal for a Council Decision on the sharing out of*

carbon dioxide emissions among Member States in order to achieve the carbon dioxide stabilisation Community target by the year 2000. Brussels, 29.5.91.

22 Commission of the European Communities (1990) *Proposal for a Council Decision concerning the promotion of energy efficiency in the Community.* COM(90) 365 final, Brussels, 13.11.90.

23 See, for example, Grubb (1989) *The Greenhouse Effect: Negotiating Targets*, London, Royal Institute of International Affairs; Nitze, (1990) *The Greenhouse Effect: Formulating a Convention*, London, Royal Institute of International Affairs.

24 Victor, D. G. (1991) 'How to slow global warming', *Nature*, 349, 7/2/91, 451–456.

25 See Grubb, *op. cit.* and (1990) *Energy Policies and the Greenhouse Effect* Volume 1: Policy Appraisal, London, Royal Institute of International Affairs.

26 General Secretariat of the Council (1990) *Meeting Document cons/Env/90/13*, Brussels 21.12.90.

27 Jackson, T. (1991) 'Least cost greenhouse planning', *Energy Policy* Jan/Feb, 35–46; Jackson, T. and Jacobs, M. (1991) 'Carbon taxes and the assumptions of environmental economics', in Barker, T. *op. cit.*

28 CCIRG, *op. cit.*.

29 In the area of climate change there is considerable potential for confusion of terminology. Adaptive response is used here in the sense of responses other than those aimed at reducing emissions or controlling atmospheric concentrations of radiative forcing agents. Thus the construction of sea defences, for example, is 'adaptive' in this sense, though in a narrower context it is sometimes referred to as a preventive policy.

30 Whittle, I. R. (1989) 'The Greenhouse effect: Lands at risk, an assessment', Paper presented at MAFF Conference of River and Coastal Engineers, Loughborough; London, MAFF.

31 CCIRG (1991) *op. cit.*

32 Kay, R. C. Clayton, K. and Vincent, C. (1990) 'The vulnerability of the UK coastline to sea level rise', in L. E. J. Roberts and R. C. Kay (eds) *The Effects of Sea Level Rise on the UK Coast* Research Report No. 7, for National Power/Power Gen, Norwich, University of East Anglia, Environmental Risk Assessment Unit, pp. 75–150.

33 *ibid*

34 For example, *ibid* and Parker, D. J. and Penning-Rowsell, E. C. (1981) 'Specialist hazard mapping: the Water Authorities' Land Drainage Surveys' *Area* 13, 2, 97–102.

35 In general, a sea defence protects low-lying land from inundation by the sea. Coastal protection involves preventing the sea from eroding higher land.

36 For details of the survey, see Whittle, I. R. (1991) *National Sea Defence Survey: NRA Sea Defence Database Survey, Phase 1, NRA Maintained Defences,* Paper presented at MAFF Conference of River and Coastal Engineers, Loughborough; London, MAFF.

37 CCIRG, *op. cit.*

38 Kay, Clayton and Vincent, *op. cit.*, p. 76.

39 Whittle, I. R. (1989) *op. cit.*

40 *ibid*

41 Bateman, I., Bateman, S., Brown, D., Doktor, P., Karas, J. H. W., Maher, A. and Turner, R. K. (1990) *Economic Appraisal of the Consequences of Climate-induced Sea Level Rise: A Case Study of East Anglia,* Final Report to MAFF, London, MAFF.

42 Doody, J. P. (1991) 'Sea defence and nature conservation: threat or opportunity?', Paper presented at Winter Meeting of Institution of Water and Environmental Management, River Engineering Section, 1st February. Peterborough, Nature Conservancy Council.

43 T. Yates, MAFF, personal communication.

44 Intergovernmental Panel on Climate Change Response Strategies Working Group, Coastal Zone Management Sub-Group (1990) *Strategies for Adaptation to Sea Level Rise,* The Netherlands, IPCC.

45 Department of the Environment (1987) *Development involving agricultural land* Circular 16/87, London DoE.

46 There has been some confusion over which defensive infrastructure might require an Environmental Assessment under schedule 2 of the *Town and Country Planning (Assessment of Environmental Effects) Regulations* 1988, for which the fundamental test determining whether an assessment is required is likelihood of a significant environmental impact. The Royal Town Planning Institute (RTPI) has recently given evidence to the Commons Environment Committee on this issue and has called for clarification: letter from P. Watts, Planning Policy Officer, RTPI, to the Environment Committee, 9.12.91.

47 CCIRG (1991) *op. cit.*

48 Alan Allison, MAFF, personal communication, 1991.

49 See, for example, Brook, D. (1990) 'Planning aspects of coastal management', London, Minerals and Land Reclamation Division, DoE; Clayton, K. (1991) 'Set in a rising sea', *National Trust Magazine,* 63, Summer, 26–27; Doody, J. P. *op. cit;* Gubbay, S. (1991) 'Coastal zone management in the UK', *Marine Update,* Spring, 1–4; Kay, R. (1990) 'Development controls on eroding coastlines', *Land Use Policy,* April, 169–172; Kay, R. (1991) 'Coping without concrete' *Town and Country Planning* January, 11–13.

50 MAFF and Department of the Environment (1982) *Development in Flood Risk Areas – Liaison Between Planning Authorities and Water Authorities,* Joint Circular 17/82, London, MAFF/DoE; re-issued in 1990.

51 Department of the Environment (1990) *Development on Unstable Land* PPG 14, London, DoE.

52 Kay, Clayton and Vincent 1990, *op. cit.*

53 Discussed in Kay, 1991, *op. cit.*

54 *ibid*

55 These bands, and possible standards of service, have been proposed by the NRA's consultants, Robertson Gould. For details, see Whittle, 1991, *op. cit.*

56 Kay, 1991, *ibid.*

57 *ibid,* p. 13.

58 J. P. Doody, Joint Nature Conservation Committee, personal communication.

59 Gubbay, 1991, *op. cit.*

60 Brook, 1990, *op. cit.*

61 In 1988, energy use for transport, amounting to some 30 per cent of total final energy demand, exceeded that of both the industrial and domestic sectors for the first time. Energy use for transport doubled in the period 1958–1988, when total UK energy use by final consumers increased by about 20 per cent. (Department of Energy (1989) *Digest of UK Energy Statistics,* London, HMSO.)

62 Secretary of State for the Environment *et al* (1990), *op. cit.*

63 Department of the Environment (1989) *op cit.*

64 Figures provided to authors by the Department of Transport, 1991.

65 Banister, D. (1991) 'Energy use, transport and settlement patterns', Paper for Regional Science Association Annual Conference, Oxford, September.

66 SERPLAN (1989) *Regional Transport Statement* RPC 1235, London, SERPLAN.

67 Banister, D. (1991) *op. cit.*

68 Department of the Environemnt (1988) *Major Retail Development,* Planning Policy Guidance Note 6, London, DoE.

69 See, for example, Champion, A. G. (1989) 'United Kingdom: population deconcentration as a cyclic phenomenon', in A. G. Champion (ed) *Counterurbanisation: The Changing Pace and Nature of Population Deconcentration,* London, Edward Arnold; Owens, S. E. (1991) *Energy-Conscious Planning,* London, Council for the Protection of Rural England; Steadman, P. (1990) *The Scope for Energy Conservation through Land Use Planning,* Report to Department of the Environment, Milton Keynes, Centre for Configurational Studies, Open University; Transnet (1990) *op. cit.*

70 There has been some downturn recently in the rate of counterurbanisation, but it is expected to recover – see Champion, A. G. (1989) *ibid.*

71 Department of Transport (1989) *op. cit.*

72 See, for example, speech by Transport Secretary Malcolm Rifkind: Department of Transport Press Release, 28.5.91.

73 Association of Metropolitan Authorities (AMA) (1990) *Changing Gear: Urban Transport Policy into the Next Century,* London, AMA.

74 The hydrogen and electricity would have to be to be derived from non-fossil sources.

75 For example, see Department of Energy (1990), *op. cit.* (EP 58); Energy Technology Support Unit (ETSU) (1989) *Energy Use and Energy Efficiency in the UK Transport Sector up to the Year 2010,* London, HMSO; Transnet (1990) *Energy, Transport and the Environment,* London, Transnet.

76 ETSU (1989) *ibid.*

77 Department of Transport (1989) *Transport Statistics, Great Britain 1978–88,* London, HMSO.

78 Earth Resources Research Ltd. (ERRL) (1989) *Atmospheric Emissions from the Use of Transport in the UK: Vol. 1, the Estimation of Current and Future Emissions,* Report for Worldwide Fund for Nature (WWF) UK Ltd., London, WWF/ERRL.

79 Maltby, D. Monteath, I. G. and Lawler, K. A. (1978) 'The UK surface passenger transport sector: energy consumption and policy options for conservation', *Energy Policy* 6, 294–313.

80 Department of Transport (1989) *op. cit.*

81 New capacity, particularly for rail systems, is expensive. To double the number of British Rail trains would cost more than the value of the current stock. New lines would be more expensive still, and maintenance and signals on existing lines would need to be improved. Environmental constraints may be considerable. Required investment might be as much as £10 bn.

82 ETSU (1989) *op. cit.*

83 Department of Transport Press Release 28.5.91.

84 Transnet (1990) *op. cit.,* p. 94.

85 *ibid.* Assumes normal consumption 35 mpg.

86 OECD (1985) *Energy Savings and Road Traffic Management,* Paris, OECD.

87 The 'Downs-Thomson paradox', discussed in more detail in Mogridge, M., Holden, D., Bird, J. and Terzis, G. (1987) 'The Downs-Thompson Paradox and the transportation planning process', *International Journal of Transport Economics,* October.

88 Department of Energy (1977) *Report of the Working Group on Energy Elasticities,* Energy Paper 17, London, HMSO; Pearson, M. and Smith, S. (1990) *Taxation and Environmental Policy: Some Initial Evidence* London, Institute for Fiscal Studies.

89 Leisure trips tend to have higher elasticities than work trips, Lewis, D. (1977) 'Estimating the influence of public policy on road traffic levels', *Journal of Transport Economics and Policy* 9, 155–168.

90 Carpenter, S. M. and Dix, M. C. (1980) 'Perceptions of motoring costs and responses to cost changes', WP–123, Oxford, Transport Studies Unit, University of Oxford; Corsi, T. M. and Harvey, M. E. (1977) 'Energy crisis travel behaviour and the transportation planning process', *Transportation Research Record* no. 648, 30–36. Short term responses to collapse of a bridge linking city and suburbs in Hobart, Australia also tend to confirm these findings, see Wood, L. J. and Lee, T. R. (1980) 'Time-space convergence: reappraisal for an oil short future' *Area* 12, 217–222.

91 Dix, M. C. and Goodwin, P. B. (1981) 'Understanding the effects of changing petrol prices: a synthesis of conflicting econometric and psychometric evidence', *Proceedings of Planning Transportation Research and Computation PTRC Annual Meeting*, Warwick, Oxford, Transport Studies Unit, University of Oxford; Mogridge, M. J. H. (1977) 'An analysis of household transport expenditures, 1971–1975', *Proceedings of Planning Transportation Research and Computation (PTRC) Annual Meeting*, London, Transport Studies Group, University College London.

92 Dix, M. C. and Goodwin, P. B. (1981) *ibid* and (1982) 'Petrol prices and car use: a synthesis of conflicting evidence', *Transport Policy Decision Making*, 2, 179–195; Marche, R. (1980) 'Rapport Intermediare', Groupe de Travail 'Demande Voyageurs', Co-operation entre Organismes Nationaux pour l'Etude des Transport Interregionaux (from Institut de Récherche de Transports, 94114 Archeuil Cedex; Bates, J. and Roberts, M. (1982) 'Forecasts for the ownership and use of a car', in *The Future of the Use of the Car*, Round Tables 55, 56 and 57, Paris, Economic Research Centre, European Conference of Ministers of Transport.

93 Hewitt, P. (1989) *A Cleaner, Faster London: Road Pricing, Transport Policy and the Environment*, Green Paper No. 1, London, Institute for Public Policy Research.

94 *ibid*

95 MVA Consultancy Report to London Planning Advisory Committee, January 1989, cited in Hewitt, P. (1989), *ibid*.

96 National transport policy, and trunk roads, are the responsibility of the Department of Transport. County Councils are responsible for other roads and for the co-ordination of transport policy at County level. Certain tasks, for example parking control, may be delegated to district councils.

97 The roads programme has been developed in two papers from the Department of Transport: Department of Transport (1989) *Roads for Prosperity* and Department of Transport (1990) *Trunk Roads, England – Into the 1990s*.

98 Automobile Association (AA) (undated) *Transport and the Environment: A Policy Statement*, Basingstoke, AA.

99 See, for example, speech by Malcolm Rifkind, *op. cit.*

100 Secretary of State for the Environment *et al* (1990) *op. cit.*

101 Netherlands Second Chamber of the States General (1989) *National Environmental Policy Plan* The Hague, The Netherlands, Ministry of Housing, Physical Planning and Environment.

102 Secretary of State for the Environment *et al* (1990) *op. cit.*

103 Netherlands Second Chamber of the States General (1989) *op. cit.*, Policy A 195c, p. 203.

104 Kent County Council (1990) *The Transport Challenge: A New Approach for Kent,* Maidstone, Kent, Highways and Transportation Department, Kent County Council, p. 27.

105 ETSU (1989) *op. cit.*

106 Hallett, S. (1990) *Drivers' Attitudes to Driving, Cars and Traffic,* Oxford, Transport Studies Unit, University of Oxford.

107 See respectively, for examples of each approach, Beaumont, J. R. and Keys, P. (1982) *Future Cities: Spatial Analysis of Energy Issues,* Chichester, John Wiley; Romanos, M. C. 'Energy price effects on metropolitan structure and form', *Environment and Planning A,* 10, 93–104; Wilson, A. G. (1981) *Catastrophe Theory and Bifurcation: Applications to Urban Regional Systems,* Beckenham, Kent, Croom Helm.

108 For a critique, see Owens, S. E. (1989) 'Models and urban energy analysis: a review and critique', in L. Lundqvist *et al* (eds) *Spatial Energy Analysis: Models for Strategic Energy Decisions in an Urban and Regional Context,* London, Gower, 227–44.

109 See, for example, Mogridge, M. (1984) Review of Beaumont and Keys, *op. cit.,* in *Progress in Human Geography* 8, 591–593, p. 592. Some recent applications of dynamical systems theory even suggest that future states of complex urban systems may be inherently unpredictable: see Wilson, A. G. (1981) *op. cit.:* for a discussion, see Owens, S. E. (1986) *Energy, Planning and Urban Form,* London, Pion.

110 See, for example, Clark, James W. (1974) *Defining an Urban Growth Strategy which will Achieve Maximum Travel Demand Reduction and Access Opportunity Enhancement,* Research Report 73 (7 UMTA WA 0003 74) Seattle, Department of Civil Engineering, Washington University; Edwards, J. L. and Schofer, J. L. (1975) *Relationships between Transportation Energy Consumption and Urban Structure: Results of Simulation Studies,* Minneapolis, MN: Department of Civil and Mineral Engineering; Roberts, J. S. (1975). 'Energy and land use: analysis of alternative development patterns', *Environmental Comment,* September, 2–11.

111 For example Keyes, D. L. 'Reducing travel and fuel use through urban planning', in R. W. Burchell and D. Listoken (eds) *Energy and Land Use,* Centre for Urban Policy Research, New Brunswick, 1982;

Newman, P. W. G. and Kenworthy, J. R. (1989) 'Gasoline consumption and cities', *APA Journal,* Winter.

112 See, for example, Clark (1974), *op. cit.;* Edwards and Schofer (1975), *op. cit.;* Fels, M. F. and Munson, M. J. (1975) 'Energy thrift in urban transportation: options for the future', in Robert H. Williams (ed) *The Energy Conservation Papers: A Report to the Energy Project of the Ford Foundation,* Cambridge, MA, Ballinger; Rickaby, P., *op. cit.* Note 36; Roberts, J. S., *op. cit.* For an assessment of this research, see Owns, S. E. (1986) *op. cit.;* and Owens, S. E. (1990) 'Land use planning for energy efficiency', in J. B. Cullingworth (ed) *Energy, Land and Public Policy,* Center for Energy and Urban Policy Research, University of Delaware, USA, Transaction Publishers, 53–98.

113 Commission of the European Communities (1990) *Green Paper on the Urban Environment,* Brussels, CEC.

114 Naess, P. (1991) 'Environment Protection by Urban Concentration', paper presented at Conference on *Housing Policy as a Strategy for Change,* Oslo, Norwegian Institute for Urban and Regional Research.

115 See for example Albert, J. D. and Banton, H. S. (1978) 'Urban spatial adjustments resulting from rising energy costs', *Annals of Regional Science* 12, 64–71; Clark (1974), *op. cit.;* Hemmens, G. (1967) 'Experiments in urban form and structure', *Highway Research Record 207, 32–41; Owens, S. E. (1981) The Energy Implications of Alternative Rural Development Patterns,* PhD Thesis, University of East Anglia, Norwich; Schneider, J. and Beck, J. (1973) *Reducing the Travel Requirements of the American City: An Investigation of Alternative Urban Spatial Structures,* Research Report 73, US Department of Transportation, Washington DC; Stone, P. A. (1973) *The Structure, Size and Costs of Urban Settlements,* Cambridge, Cambridge University Press; Romanos, M. C. (1978) *op. cit.*

116 Kent County Council (1991) *op. cit.,* p. 17.

117 Breheny, M., 'Strategic planning and urban sustainability', paper presented to Town and Country Planning Association Conference on *Planning for Sustainable Development,* London, 27–28th November 1990.

118 Rickaby, P. (1987) 'Six settlement patterns compared', *Environment and Planning B, Planning and Design,* 14, 192–223.

119 Keyes, D. L. and Peterson, G. (1977) *Urban Development and Energy Consumption,* Working Paper No. 5049, Washington DC, Urban Land Institute.

120 Roberts, J. S. (1975) *op. cit.;* Jamieson, G., Mackay, W. and Latchford, J. (1967) 'Transportation and land use structures', *Urban Studies,* 4, 201–217.

121 Netherlands Ministry of Housing, Physical Planning and the Environment, *On the road to 2015,* (Summary of Fourth Report on Physical Planning in the Netherlands). The Hague, Ministry of Housing, Physical Planning and the Environment, p. 21.

122 Barton, H. (1987) *The Potential for Increasing the Energy Efficiency of Existing Urban Areas through Local Planning Policy,* M. Phil Thesis, Department of Town and Country Planning, Bristol Polytechnic; Steadman, P. (1980) *Configurations of Land Uses, Transport Networks and their Relation to Energy Use,* Centre for Configurational Studies, Open University, Milton Keynes.

123 Netherlands Ministry of Housing, Physical Planning and the Environment (1990) *National Environmental Policy Plan Plus,* English Version, The Hague, Ministry of Housing etc., Department of Information and International Relations, p. 53.

124 *ibid,* p. 13.

125 *ibid,* p. 53.

126 Netherlands Ministry of Housing, Physical Planning and the Environment (1990) *Report on Physical Planning and Spatial Policy 1989/90,* The Hague, Ministry of Housing etc.

127 Fritsche, U. (1990) *Urban Energy Management: Local Strategies for Ecological Improvement,* Paper prepared for the OECD Environment Directorate, Urban Affairs Division, October.

128 For a description of TRANUS, see Rickaby, P. (1987) *op. cit.*

129 Confidential memo circulated by UK Government, cited in Hughes, P. (1991) *op. cit.,* reference BBC Television Newsnight, October 1990.

130 Secretary of State for the Environment *et al, op. cit.,* p. 76.

131 *ibid,* p. 87.

132 Memorandum submitted by the Combined Heat and Power Association to the House of Commons Energy Committee, *op. cit.,* Vol. II, pp. 56–61.

133 Department of Energy (1989) *An Evaluation of Energy-Related Greenhouse Gas Emissions and Measures to Ameliorate them,* Energy Paper 58, London, HMSO, para 5.4.1.

134 *ibid*

135 *ibid* and House of Commons Energy Committee (1991) *Energy Efficiency,* Third Report, Session 1990–91, 91–I, London, HMSO.

136 Newcastle-upon-Tyne City Council, Case Study of CHP, undated Working Paper.

137 See, for example, CHP Group, *District Heating combined with Electricity Generation in the United Kingdom,* Energy Paper 20, HMSO, London, 1977; and *Combined Heat and Electrical Power Generation in the United Kingdom,* Energy Paper 35, HMSO, London, 1979.

138 CHP Association, *op. cit.*

139 Sheffield Heat and Power (SHP) undated Information Package, Sheffield, SHP.

140 Burdon, I. P. (1990) *CHP on Tyneside – The Forth Energy Project: A Description of the Scheme,* Newcastle-upon-Tyne, Merz and Mclellan Consulting Engineers.

141 D. Green, CHP Association, personal communication.

142 Knudsen, J. E. and Ricken, J. H. (1989) 'Development of Danish Combined Heat and Power Systems', Paper presented at 14th Congress of the World Energy Conference, Division 2, *Energy and the Environment,* Montreal, 17–22 September.

143 Danish Ministry of Energy (1987) *District Heating in Denmark* Copenhagen, Danish Ministry of Energy.

144 A feature of the organisation of the privatised electricity generation system in the UK is a government-imposed requirement on the Regional Electricity Companies to purchase a proportion of their electricity supplies from non-fossil sources. Waste combustion and landfill gas technologies are classified as non-fossil.

145 House of Commons Energy Committee, *op. cit.,* para 73.

146 Existing capacity in the industrial sector (1.8 GWe) could at least double in the 1990s on current trends (CHP Association). Prospects for building (or commercial) CHP are good: a market review by the Energy Technology Support Unit has identified at least 4,000 sites (including hotels, hospitals, grouped accommodation, swimming pools, leisure centres and office complexes) – equivalent to some 320 MWe (eight times current capacity in this area) – where package CHP systems could be used. Simple extrapolation suggests that about 1 GWe might be installed during the 1990s.

147 Burdon, *op. cit.*

148 This was cited among benefits of a recent group heating scheme in the London Borough of Waltham Forest. See Energy Efficiency Office (1989) *Combined Heat and Power Plant for Group Heating in Domestic Housing,* Case Study 21, London, Department of Energy.

149 Select Committee on Energy, *op. cit.,* para 76. The Government has rejected the NFFO/FFL proposal.

150 CHP Association, *op. cit.,* para 29.1.

151 House of Commons Energy Committee, *op. cit.,* para 77.

152 CHP Group, *op. cit.*

153 W. S. Atkins and Partners (1982) *CHP/DH Feasibility Programme: Stage 1, Summary Report and Recommendations for the Department of Energy,* Epsom, Surrey, W. S. Atkins and Partners.

154 Assuming CHP from two small back pressure sets, which utilise heat from the steam exhaust.

155 W. S. Atkins and Partners, *op. cit.*

156 D. Green, CHP Association, personal communication, 1991.

157 In Denmark, under the 1979 Heat Supply Act, town councils have the right to stipulate that all potential consumers of district heating must be connected: in Kalundborg, for example, this right was exercised in 1984, requiring connection by 1993. (See Danish Ministry of Energy, *op. cit.*

158 Burdon, *op. cit.*

159 Danish Ministry of Energy, *op. cit.,* p. 43.

160 Department of Energy *op. cit.,* (EP 58).

161 *ibid.* The order under the NFFO was issued on October 31 1991. Department of Energy, SI 1991, 2490.

162 Extract from Inspector's Report of the Inquiry into an application by Wind Energy Group Ltd. to construct 24 wind generators at Cemmaes, Powys, appended to Welsh Office decision letter 19.9.91. Cardiff, Welsh Office.

163 Manning, M I. (1990) Environmental Aspects of Wind Turbines, Imperial College, July. London, National Power.

164 The Inspector at the public inquiry into the Cemmaes wind farm, held in April 1990, suggested that the total developed area for 24 generators, including access track, would be some 2.27 ha, whereas the site area is 325 ha. Each wind turbine generator requires a seven metre diameter concrete base.

165 Extract from Inspector's Report of the Inquiry into an application by Wind Energy Group Ltd. to construct 24 wind generators at Cemmaes, Powys, *op. cit.,* p. 39.

166 Objectors at the Cemmaes inquiry made this point. See *ibid.*

167 Secretary of State for the Environment *et al, op. cit.,* para C 13.

168 These are some uncertainties surrounding the exact figure. The estimate of 27 per cent is from Jackson, T. and Roberts, S. (1989) *Getting Out of the Greenhouse,* London, Friends of the Earth. A slightly lower estimate of around 23 per cent has been made by the Building Research Establishment (BRE) (The Greenhouse Effect, *Building Services,* July 1989, p. 65) BRE suggest that a figure of around 25 per cent would reflect these uncertainties (L. Shorrock, personal communication, 1991).

169 According to Energy Paper 58 *op. cit.,* the domestic sector is responsible for about 28 per cent of UK carbon dioxide emissions (1987 figures, including emissions from energy conversion). Space heating accounts for 60 per cent of domestic energy use, but for less than half of the carbon dioxide emissions (around 45 per cent), because of the preponderance of gas in this market.

170 *ibid*

171 Barnes, D. and Rankin, L. (1975) 'The energy economics of building construction', *Building International* 8, 31–42; Building Research Establishment (1975) *Energy Conservation; A Study of Energy Con-*

sumption in Buildings and Means of Saving Energy in Housing, Current Paper 56, Watford, UK, Building Research Establishment; Brooke, J. (1991) 'A housing manager's guide to saving the planet', Housing, 27, 1, 14–17, February.

172 Grot, R. A. and Socolow, R. H. (1973) Energy Utilization in a Residential Community, Working Paper W–7, Princeton, Princeton University Center for Environmental Studies; Loudon, A. and Cornish, P. (1975). 'Thermal insulation studies', Building Research Establishment News, No. 4, p. 4.

173 Department of the Environment (1988) 1985-based Estimates of Numbers of Households 1985–2001, London, DoE.

174 NBA Tectonics (1988) A Study of Passive Solar Housing Estate Layout London, Department of Energy.

175 ibid

176 Building Research Establishment (1990) Climate and Site Development Digest 350 (three parts), Watford, BRE; Keeble, E. J., Collins, M. and Ryser, J. (1989) 'The potential of land use planning and development control to help achieve favourable microclimates around buildings: a European review', Paper to CIB/IFHP/WMO Conference, Kyoto, Japan, November, available from Building Research Establishment, Garston, Watford, Herts.

177 Lamm, J. O. (1986) Energy in Physical Planning: A Method for Developing the Municipality Master Plan with Regard to Energy Criteria, Document D14:1986, Stockholm, Sweden, Swedish Council for Building Research.

178 Building Research Establishment (BRE) (1990) op. cit.; Property Services Agency (PSA) (1988) Energy Saving through Landscape Planning, PSA.

179 Keeble et al, op. cit.

180 The survey, of all strategic planning authorities and a sample of and a sample of districts, London boroughs and metropolitan authorities is reported in Owens, S. E. (1991) Energy-Conscious Planning London, Council for the Protection of Rural England.

181 Department of the Environment et al, op. cit., para C 40).

182 NBA Tectonics (1988) op. cit.

183 House of Commons Energy Committee, op. cit., para 106.

184 House of Commons Energy Committee (1991) Government Observations on the Third Report from the Committee (Session 1990–91) on Energy Efficiency Fifth Special Report, London, HMSO.

185 Owens (1991), op. cit.

186 Bergman, L. (1976) An Energy Demand Model for the Swedish Residential Sector, Document D4 1976, Stockholm, Sweden, Swedish Council for Building Research; Lundqvist, L. (1989) 'A model system for strategic metropolitan energy studies', in L. Lundqvist, L-G Mattson and E. A. Erikson (eds) Spatial Energy Analysis: Models for Strategic Decisions in an Urban and Regional Context, Aldershot, UK, Gower; Wene, C-O. and Ryden, B. (1988) 'A comprehensive energy model in the municipal energy planning process', European Journal of Operational Research, 33, 212.

187 'Least cost planning', pioneered by US electricity utilities within a tight regulatory framework, essentially treats on an equal basis investment in new supply facilities and investment in improving energy efficiency.

188 Because such systems still burn coal, the contribution arises solely from their improved thermal-electrical energy conversion efficiency. British Gas, in 1989 evidence to the House of Commons Energy Select Committee, gave a figure of only a 5 per cent improvement over new conventional coal-fired stations for a coal-using gasification combined cycle system with advanced gas turbines. See HMSO (1989) op. cit.

189 Removing carbon dioxide from the flue gases of fossil-fuelled plant by absorption in organic solvents followed by thermal stripping or by cryogenic technologies. In the UK case, the most likely isolation option would be injection into depleted oil and gas reservoirs, most probably in the North Sea. Any scheme would therefore involve pipeline and associated infrastructure. Use for enhanced recovery from existing oil fields could improve the economics but the amounts of carbon dioxide that could, on a very long term basis, be used in this way are uncertain.

190 Department of Energy (1989) op. cit.

191 CEGB (1989), Memorandum of Evidence to House of Commons Select Committee on Energy, op. cit.

192 Financial Times Business Information, 1991.

193 No data are presented in Energy Paper 58 on the capacity of existing plant that might be retired under different new-build assumptions, but it might be reasonable to assume the closure of all existing coal-fired stations of under 400MWe capacity. This is made the more likely because, independent of an accentuated gas-coal substitution programme, the post-CEGB generators are involved in a vigorous programme of generating station closure.

194 Eyre, (1991) 'The gaseous emissions due to electricity fuel cycles in the UK', Energy and Environment, 2, 2, 167–181.

195 Department of Energy (1991) Proof of Evidence to Kirkby Moor Wind Farm Public Inquiry, May.

196 Taylor, E. H. (1990) Review of Photovoltaic Power Technology ETSU-R-50, London, HMSO.

197 Central Electricity Generating Board, undated.

198 'Future looks brighter for UK's nuclear industry', Independent on Sunday 6.10.91.

199 This experience is reviewed in detail in Owens, S. E. (1985) 'Energy, participation and planning: the case of electricity generation in Great Britain', in

Calzonetti, F. J. and Soloman, B. (eds) *Geographical Dimensions of Energy*, Dordrecht, Reidel, 225–254.

200 Owens, S. E. (1985) *op. cit.* Such considerations would be likely to include the need for control of other developments in the vicinity of nuclear installations.

201 National Rivers Authority (1991) *Demands and Resources of Water Undertakers in England and Wales* Preliminary Report Under Section 143 (2) (a) ater Act 1989, London (now Bristol), NRA.

202 *ibid*, p. 1.

203 *ibid*, p. 8.

204 CCIRG, (1991) *op. cit.* p. 60.

205 Parry 1989, *op. cit.*

206 Potential effects are summarised by the CCIRG 1990, *op. cit.* See also Squire, G. R. and Unsworth, M. H. (1988) *Effects of CO$_2$ Climate Change on Agriculture,* Report to UK Department of the Environment, University of Nottingham; Parry, M. (1989) 'Potential impacts of climate change in the UK', *Soil and Water Management,* Winter 1989, 124–125; Institute of Terrestrial Ecology (1989), Review of the mild winter 1988–89 in *ENDS Report* 179; Armstrong, A. C. and Castle, D. A. (1989) 'Climate change and field drainage', *Soil and Water Management,* Winter, 126–127;

207 CCIRG, (1991) *op. cit.* p. 43.

208 MacGuire, F. and Barkham, J. (1990) 'Sea level rise and coastal ecology', in L. E. J. Roberts and R. C. Kay (eds) *The Effects of Sea Level Rise on the UK Coast,* Research Report Number 7 for National Power/Power Gen, Norwich, Environmental Risk Assessment Unit, University of East Anglia.

209 Rifkind, M. (1987) Statement by the Secretary of State for Scotland in the House of Commons, 23.10.87.

210 See, for example, Anderson, D. (1991) *The Forestry Industry and the Greenhouse Effect* A Report for the Scottish Forestry Trust and the Forestry Commission, Edinburgh, Scottish Forestry Trust/Forestry Commission; Kayes, R. J., Arden-Clarke, C. and Taylor, P. J. (1990) *An Assessment of the Feasibility of Large-Scale Afforestation in Britain to Offset Carbon Dioxide Emissions,* Report prepared for the National Power Division of the Central Electricity Generating Board. Oxford, Political Ecology Research Group.

211 Secretary of State for the Environment *et al, op. cit.*

212 *ibid*

213 As a tree grows, it both absorbs and respires carbon dioxide, with the net balance favouring accumulation of carbon, until the tree is mature. When the timber decomposes, the carbon fixed by trees is returned to the atmosphere, but this occurs slowly and, for trees planted now, not until at least forty years into the future. If the timber is converted into durable products, then the release of carbon dioxide can be lagged for a considerable time.

214 If the entire non-urban, unforested area of the UK area were planted, the trees might sequester up to 40 MtC per year once established, continuing until maturity (total emissions in 1987 were 156 MtC). However, only a small proportion of this area could realistically be afforested.

215 'Britain juggles green controls', *Guardian* 28.5.91.

216 A good summary of existing schemes can be found in Kayes *et al, op. cit.*

217 Countryside Commission (1990). *The New National Forest* Cheltenham, The Countryside Commission; see also Kayes *et al, op. cit.*

218 Kayes *et al.* (1990) *op. cit.*

219 Kayes *et al.* (1990) *op. cit.*

220 CCIRG p. 45.

221 *This Common Inheritance*, 6.15–6.17; these changes, essentially applying nationwide legislative powers already existing in the National Parks, are implemented in the Planning and Compensation Act.

222 Potentially damaging operations in SSSIs and National Parks are notifiable to the Nature Conservation Councils and National Park Authorities respectively and there is provision for voluntary management agreements and payments. In Environmentally Sensitive Areas there is a system of incentive payments to encourage farmers to use traditional practices to protect landscape and wildlife. In the forestry sector, new planting proposals are referred by the Forestry Commission to MAFF, to the Nature Conservation Councils, and to National Parks Authorities and local authorities for an amenity appraisal. If objections cannot be resolved by discussion, the case is referred to the appropriate Regional Advisory Committee.

223 Speech by Sir George Young, Minister for Housing and Planning, at TCPS Summer School, 11.9.91. (Draft PPG issued February 1992).

224 Scottish Development Department (1990) *Indicative Forestry Strategies,* Circular No. 13/1990, Edinburgh, Scottish Development Department; see also Hampson, A. (1991) 'Where to put the forests', UKCEED *Bulletin*, No. 32.

225 C. Fuller, (I.E.A.), personal communication, 29.5.91.

226 Currently it is intended that some parts of the community forest could be planned in some detail, such as areas of local authority land, or parts of farms to be devoted immediately to the project. For other areas it might only be possible to ascribe broad themes to be realised in the future. The zoning of the plan should encompass different time scales, and different degrees of flexibility.

227 Countryside Commission (1990) *Advice Manual for the Preparation of a Community Forest Plan*, Cheltenham, The Countryside Commission, p. 20.

228 Department of the Environment (1988) *General Policy and Principles* PPG 1, January, London DoE.

229 CPRE (1991) Press Release, *Community Forest Charter*, 29th May, London, CPRE.

230 *ibid*

231 Ratcliffe, D. (1977). *A Nature Conservation Review,* Peterborough, NCC.

232 Andrew Farmer, English Nature, personal communication, 1991.

233 Doody, personal communication.

234 Smith, J. B. and Tirpak, D. (1989) *The Potential Effects of Climate Change on the United States* Report to Congress, US Environmental Protection Agency, Planning and Evaluation Office of Research and Development. Washington DC, US EPA.

235 Parry, M. (1990) *Climate Change and World Agriculture,* London, Earthscan.

236 Anderson, D. *op. cit.*

237 Unpublished report by David Pearce *et al.,* reviewed in *The Observer* 12.5.91. The cost-benefit analysis did not attempt to value amenity. Kayes *et al.* (1990) *op. cit.* have questioned the difference in carbon assimilation rates between conifers and broadleaved trees.

238 Congress of the US Office of Technology Assessment (OTA) (1991) *Changing by Degrees.* Washington DC, OTA.

239 *ibid,* p. 59.

240 CCIRG recommendation, 5.5.2 (i) and (ii).

241 See, for example, Harvey (1991) *The CAP and Green Agriculture,* London, Institute for Public Policy Research; Jenkins, (1991), CPRE.

242 Department of Energy and Department of the Environment Press Release, 1991. (Draft PPG issued December 1991).

243 Speech by Sir George Young, Minister for Housing and Planning, at TCPS Summer School, 11.9.91.

244 House of Commons Select Committee on Energy (1991) *op. cit.*

APPENDIX 1

Acronyms

bau   business as usual

CAP   Common Agricultural Policy

CCGT   Combined cycle gas turbine

CCIRG   (UK) Climate Change Impacts Review Group

CEGB   Central Electricity Generating Board

CFC   Chlorofluorocarbon

CHP   Combined heat and power

CO_2 Carbon dioxide

DH   District heating

DoE   Department of the Environment

EA   Environmental assessment

EP 58   Energy Paper 58

ESRC   Economic and Social Research Council

ESI   Electricity supply industry

ETSU   Energy Technology Support Unit

FFL   Fossil fuel levy

GCM   Global circulation model (sometimes global climate model)

GW/GWh   Gigawatt/Gigawatt hour (Giga = 10^9)

Ha   Hectare

ICSU   International Council of Scientific Unions

IPCC   Intergovernmental Panel on Climate Change

LRT   Light rapid transit

LWR   Light water reactor

MAFF   Ministry of Agriculture, Fisheries and Foods

MW/MWh   Megawatt/Megawatt hour (Mega = 10^6)

mtc	Million tonnes of carbon
mtce	Million tonnes of carbon equivalent
NFFO	Non-fossil fuel obligation
NNR	Notified nature reserve
NO_x	Oxides of nitrogen
NRA	National Rivers Authority
OFFER	Office of Electricity Regulation
PPG	Planning policy guidance
PV	Photovoltatic
PWR	Pressurised water reactor
Rfg	Radiative forcing gas
SSSI	Site of Special Scientific Interest
TW/TWh	Terawatt/Terawatt hour (Tera = 10^{12})
UEA	University of East Anglia
UNCED	United Nations Conference on Environment and Development (1992)
UNEP	United Nations Environment Programme
WMO	World Meteorological Organisation
WWF	Worldwilde Fund for Nature

APPENDIX 2

List of Contacts

Discussions were held with, or information provided by, the following organisations and individuals during the course of the desk study. *denotes a member of the Steering Group.

Anglian Water plc
                                        Mr. D. Latham
                                        Mr. P. Stott
Building Research Establishment   Dr. E. Keeble
Climate Change Impacts Review Group   Professor J. K. Page
Combined Heat and Power Association   Mr. D. Green
Countryside Commission   Rick Minter
                                        Ian Mitchell
Department of Energy   Dr. David Evans
Department of the Environment
    Directorate of Planning Services   Mr. M. Bach*
    Global Atmosphere Division   Dr. J. Fisher*
                                        Dr. J. Penman*
Department of Transport   Alan Nicholls
                                        John Rickard
Energy Technology Support Unit   Dr. K. Currie
                                        Dr. N. Eyre
English Nature   Andrew Farmer
Hadley Centre   Dr. Bennetts
                                        Dr. P. Rowntree
Joint Nature Conservation Committee   Dr. J. P. Doody
London Boroughs Association   David Hurdle
Ministry of Agriculture, Fisheries and Foods   Mr. A. Allison*
                                        Mr. T. Yates*
National Rivers Authority   Ian Whittle
National Power   Dr. M. L. Manning
                                        Andrew Crane
Newcastle City Council   Mr. A. Smith

APPENDIX 3

Further Details on Production of Climate Change Scenarios

IPCC Working Group I

Most GCMs operate by providing information on 'equilibrium climate sensitivity' – the temperature change resulting from an assumed increase (usually a doubling) of atmospheric radiative forcing gas concentrations (in carbon dioxide equivalent). WG I also used models which considered ocean-atmosphere interactions.

Additionally, WG I looked at information from research on past climatic regimes but concluded that 'analogues of future greenhouse-gas-changed climates have not been found' and argued against a direct predictive role for paleoclimatological research.

To derive scenarios of future climatic circumstances, WG I needed assumptions about future trends in emissions of radiative forcing gases. These were derived from four scenarios constructed by Working Group III (WG III) of the IPCC (Response Strategies), taking into account emissions of all radiative forcing gases from the present to 2100. Assumed rates of population and economic growth in the developed and developing worlds were common to all four scenarios, which otherwise varied as follows:

'Business as usual' – energy supply coal intensive, modest improvements in energy efficiency, continuing tropical forest depletion, no controls on agricultural emissions of methane and nitrous oxide, partial implementation of Montreal CFC Protocol;

'B' shift to natural gas, deforestation reversed, full implementation of Montreal CFC Protocol;

'C' shift to renewable and nuclear energy sources in second half of next century, CFCs phased out, agricultural emissions 'limited'; and

'D' shift to renewables and nuclear energy sources in first half of next century, stringent controls in developed countries and moderated emissions in developing countries.

CCIRG

The CCIRG, which mainly considered circumstances only up to 2050, unlike the 2100 range of the IPCC study, derived its scenarios of future UK climatic regimes by averaging the spatial results of five equilibrium GCMs. These were first standardised to common 5 degree grid squares. Onto this mean spatial pattern were then 'mapped' time-dependent global mean temperature changes derived from a simpler dynamic model including oceanic upwelling-diffusion effects and energy balances.

As the CCIRG noted:

'the big assumptions in this procedure are: that the average of five GCM results is a better representation of reality than any single model result, and that under continuous greenhouse forcing changes, the spatial patterns will not vary through time 'on the way' to the equilibrium condition – an unlikely situation, but the best that can be assumed at present'.[1]

The CCIRG used the same model of changes in temperature values as the IPCC WG I but different assumptions about trends in radiative forcing gas emissions. A 'business as usual' scenario alone was

---

[1] CCIRG, 1991, *op. cit.*

constructed by the Group (i.e. it did not consider the effect of adoption of any emission reduction strategies on a global scale). The main assumptions behind this net emissions scenario were:

- 1.5 per cent annual increase in fossil fuel radiative forcing gas emission throughout the period;

- unchanged rate of deforestation throughout the period; and

- application of the 1987 Montreal Protocol on CFCs, with substitution by non-radiative forcing gas alternatives.

APPENDIX 4

Summary tables of links between climate change and land use planning in initial areas of investigation.

Land use planning sensitivities to preventive responses: summary

Response/ policy	Potential emissions abatement	Likelihood of being pursued	Strength of link with land use planning	Critical time thresholds	Mode of land use planning system response	Evaluation/priorities for further work
Gas substitution in power generation	<45% reduction per KWh; nationally c.32mtC pa by 2005 (high energy price)	strong in all scenarios; may be constrained by rising gas prices	weak; consent required (deemed planning permission); extensive capacity on existing sites	short lead times – c. 3 years; lifetime c. 15 years	mainly reactive to specific proposals	no major novel issues for land use planning
More efficient coal combustion	small	small	weak	5–10 years to develop and deploy technology	unlikely to put pressure on land use planning system	none at present
Increased nuclear	virtually no emissions in operation; possibly 6–9 mtC pa by 2005, 40–70 mtC pa by 2020	contentious Govt. review in 1994	strong procedural links through public inquiry system; possible siting difficulties	1994 review; lead times < 15 years	mainly reactive to specific proposals	pending outcome of 1994 review: no urgent priorities
Wind (onshore)	modest; possibly 5 mtC pa by 2005, 11 mtC pa by 2020	increasing; moderate in enhanced emissions reduction scenario	strong because of visual impact and extensive land requirements: 37,500 ha/GW	construction time short; planning lead times medium (<5 years?)	currently reactive; potentially proactive role in no regrets/ enhanced emissions reduction scenarios	Potential conflict/ complementarity with other land uses merits examination. Planning guidance forthcoming[242]: effectiveness should be monitored Proactive role of planning authorities in identifying suitable areas should be explored

continued

Response/ policy	Potential emissions abatement	Likelihood of being pursued	Strength of link with land use planning	Critical time thresholds	Mode of land use planning system response	Evaluation/priorities for further work
Tidal	modest; c. 5 mtC pa if Severn and Mersey barrages constructed	small because of capital constraints except in enhanced emissions reduction scenario	strong procedural links; significant environmental impacts; also regional development implications	lead times of <15 years	primarily reactive	raises many site specific issues; also has regional development implications; otherwise few generic planning policy issues or research needs
Biomass	small/ uncertain	probably small in all scenarios	currently weak, though strong links to *land use*	medium-long timescale for development	currently weak (see agriculture/ forestry)	Limited remit of land use planning system in relation to agriculture and forestry implies few immediate research needs
Waste incineration/ landfill gas	landfill gas, small; perhaps 0.6 mtC pa by 2020; waste incineration uncertain:	high in both cases, even in bau scenario	strong: landfill siting and location of incineration facilities	short for landfill gas; uncertain for incineration because of planning constraints	proactive for landfill; mainly reactive for incineration	Potential for integrated regional waste management strategies merits some investigation.
CHP/DH	<60% reduction per KWh; technical potential – 15% reduction nationally by 2020	low-moderate for urban-scale schemes except under enhanced emissions reduction scenario	moderate-strong for urban-scale schemes; site requirements and urban structure	12–15 year lead times, urban-scale; timescale for renewal of urban infrastructure significant for coordination	mainly reactive; increasingly proactive with higher levels of response	Land use planning may enhance cost-effectiveness; opportunity costs to be explored; may be pressure for greater integration of land use and energy planning.
Modal shift	<15% energy & CO_2 savings, medium to long term	moderate, for modest measures; strong complementarity but political constraints	Strong infrastructure requirements; land use/ transport interaction	lead times for new infrastructure (10–15 years?); long term impacts of fiscal policies (10 years?)	reactive and proactive; policy instrument	Key area because of complementarity, long term significance and potentially proactive role of land use planning system. Uncertainty and lead times suggest research/policy formulation required in short term
Need to travel	uncertain, perhaps energy savings <60%	uncertain, probably increasing (already declared aim of many structure plans)	Strong land use/transport interaction	also depends on rate of change of urban infrastructure (<50 years?)		
Buildings (energy-conscious design)	c. 20% for specific developments nationally, small and long term (0.1 mtC pa after 20 years?)	slow diffusion under bau; moderate-high under other scenarios (modest benefits but little or no cost)	Strong; impact on design, layout, density etc.	turnover of building stock, c. 1% pa; regional variations	currently mainly reactive; proactive and policy instrument with higher levels of response	CO_2 abatement potential modest, but strong complementarity and few costs; land use planning system likely policy instrument; need for better understanding of constraints on translating theory into planning practice

continued

continuation of Table on p. 106

Response/ policy	Potential emissions abatement	Likelihood of being pursued	Strength of link with land use planning	Critical time thresholds	Mode of land use planning system response	Evaluation/priorities for further work
Afforestation	small c. 3 mtC pa?	moderate-high, but not primarily to abate CO_2 emissions	moderate, but largely independent of climate change	30–100 years for trees to mature	currently weak for many schemes, but active cooperation for community and national forests	carbon fixing likely to provide marginal extra justification but not to be major consideration; projects have land use planning implications but not arising from climate change

Land use planning sensitivities to adaptive responses: summary

Response/policy	Likely degree of response	Strength of link with land use planning	Critical time thresholds	Mode of land use planning	Comments and Research priorities
Response to increased flood/ erosion hazard	strong pressures for *status quo* scenario but costs under higher SLR may demand enhanced adaptive response, selective protection, adaptation and retreat	weak in *status quo* scenario (reactive to improved defences); increasing over time in bau scenario; strong in enhanced adaptive response	lifetime of hard defences <100 yrs, soft defences 30–50 yrs; renewal on rolling 5 year programme; new survey will reveal current remaining lifetimes lifetime of assets in hazard zone also significant, 50–100 years?	currently limited and reactive with some development control; enhanced adaptive response would involve land use planning as policy instrument; increasing pressures for greater coordination in coastal zone management	Very complex area with many uncertainties and strong political pressures. Need further exploration of: impacts of improved defences; role of development control in internalising risk; costs and benefits of integrated coastal zone management
Response to changes in balance between water supply and demand	very uncertain because direction of change not known; most likely response to bring forward decisions	generally weak but strong in case of reservoir development; not very sensitive to climate change	10–15 years lead time for reservoirs; supply/demand projections to 2011	limited for most supply options; possible wider planning function in spatial management of demand	Land use planning implications very uncertain in this case; probably too soon to identify coherent research requirements.
Changes in the agricultural/ forestry sectors	change in short-medium term dominated by other factors (eg CAP); longer term adaptive response may involve land use change	weak in bau and *status quo* scenarios; stronger under enhanced adaptive response because of policy coordination	extremely uncertain	currently very limited though EA may have increasing role; more proactive in longer term in context of coordination of policies for rural land use management	Very uncertain impacts, significance of other factors and currently limited remit of land use planning system in relation to agriculture and forestry implies few immediate research needs specific to climate change
Protection of NNRs	Pressures for conservation likely to increase but significant policy response to climate change unlikely in short term	Weak in bau and *status quo* scenarios; stronger with enhanced adaptive response	extremely uncertain	limited (protection from development) in bau and *status quo* scenarios; proactive with possible institutional change in enhanced adaptive response	Debate will focus on merits of protection of *status quo* versus facilitating change: implications of considering change to be a benefit merit investigation. Costs and benefits of options for allowing landward migration of coastal ecosystems, including planning controls and conditions, worth investigating

Printed in the United Kingdom for HMSO
Dd295804 4/92 C17 G531 10170